THE COMPLETE NINJA FOODI COOKBOOK FOR UK

Enjoy the Classic British Favourites with Ninja Foodi Smartlid Multi-Cooker, Colour Printed Cookbook with Pictures and 28-Day Meal Plan for Beginners

HARRIET BOLTON

LEGAL & DISCLAIMER

The content and information in this book is consistent and truthful, and it has been provided for informational, educational and business purposes only.
The content and information contained in this book has been compiled from reliable sources, which are accurate based on the knowledge, belief, expertise and information of the Author. The author cannot be held liable for any omissions and/or errors.

TABLE OF CONTENT

INTRODUCTION

Smart cooking is not made possible with the newest Ninja Shark kitchen technology, which offers you the 11-in-1 Multi Cooker with a Smart lid. In this pressure cooker, the company has combined a number of cooking options in one single appliance. It is a genuinely multifunctional kitchen equipment. There isn't much that this tabletop cooker can't do with its three different modes and 11 various culinary operations, which include slow cooking, air frying, and steaming. It even includes two brand-new "combi steam" settings that combine light steaming with conventional baking and air frying to create fluffier cakes and more succulent meats. There are endless options to cook using the Ninja Foodi Smart Lid Cooker, and this cookbook is your doorway to those flavour some ideas. The recipes here are not only delicious, but they are also created to make your Ninja Foodi cooking experience better than ever. All the recipes have easy-to-follow instructions, cooking tips, and irresistible pictures of the prepared meals. So let's try them out!

CHAPTER 1 FUNDAMENTALS OF NINJA FOODI SMART LID COOKER

It is a truly modern multi cooker with a sharp, digital display, chic, inset buttons, and a covert control dial. A sizable slider above the digital display allows you to easily move between the pressure cooking, steaming, and air frying modes, and the stylish new design eliminates the need to switch lids when using the pressure features.

This model includes 11 various cooking functions, as the name could imply, enabling you to prepare a wide range of dishes. These include slow cooking, dehydrating food, air frying, air steaming, grilling, baking, sauteing, and pressure cooking. Additionally, two "combi steam" modes like steam air frying and steam baking are available. These modes are intended to help maintain moisture without compromising crispiness. The food can also be kept warm by using the keep warm setting.

BENEFITS OF NINJA FOODI SMART LID COOKER

The multicooker, a separate air fryer basket, and a steam rack are all included in the box. If you're new to using this kind of multicooker, there is also a really useful recipe booklet that will walk you through the many modes and features and help you get the best results.

* *Capacious*

The Ninja's 6-litre (6.34 quartz) capacity makes it the perfect size for singles, couples, and families with only one child. It is somewhat large at 36 cm in diameter and 33 cm in height, but it fits even the smallest kitchen worktops.

* *Multifunctional*

One of the most flexible tabletop cookers available is the Ninja Foodi 11-in-1. It can air fry, steam fry, bake cakes in a steam oven, and slow cook in addition to pressure cooking, steaming, and slow cooking. Like the Sage, it can also create homemade yoghurt.

* *Effective Heating*

You can see a sizable heating element right behind the cover if you lift it. For the air-frying and roasting settings, use this. It has a removable 6-liter cooking pot, and it is also non-stick, which makes cleaning it considerably simpler. Additionally, Ninja offers a crisper bowl for use with the air fry feature and a foldable wire rack for use with steaming.

* *Smart Lid Slider*

The 'Smart Lid Slider' on the Ninja Foodi 11-in-1 has three locations, each of which can be used to select one of the three primary cooking modes: pressure cooking, combi-steaming, and air frying and stovetop modes. The extreme left position is for pressure mode, the middle one is for combi-steam, and the last one is for air fry and stove top mode.

* *Modes and Sub-Modes*

On the interface, each cooking mode displays a separate set of submenus. For instance, the Combi-Steam function offers Steam Air Fry and Steam Bake as two different types of cooking processes.

The Air Fry/Hob mode offers an even greater selection of cooking techniques, including Air Fry, Grill, Bake, Dehydrate, Sear/Sauté, Steam Slow Cook, and Yoghurt, whereas the Pressure function only allows for pressure cooking and securely locks the lid.
You can adjust the cooking temperature and time defaults for each sub-setting as well. I simply left everything at default settings and opened the lid every so often to see how the food was doing. It was a little perplexing at first, but as long as I followed the instructions and used the tip sheet that came with it, I eventually figured it out.

UNDERSTANDING THE CONTROL PANEL

The multicooker, a separate air fryer basket, and a steam rack are all included in the box. If you're new to using this kind of multicooker, there is also a really useful recipe booklet that will walk you through the many modes and features and help you get the best results.

* SMARTLID SLIDER:

The Smart Lid Slider has three positions. Different sets of functions are controlled by each place. To swiftly relieve pressure or set up a delayed release, push the Pressure, Combi-Steam Mode, and Air Fry/Hob Release Pressure buttons. This won't light up until the Pressure function starts.

* Left arrows:

When using the digital cooking probe, press the "up and down" arrow key to the left of the display to change the cooking temperature or result.

* Preset:

Press the Preset button to use the digital cooking probe to precisely cook the meat or fish to your preferences.

* Manual:

The Manual button changes the display screen so you can manually set the probe's internal result.

* START/STOP:

Press the Start/Stop button to begin cooking. The current function will be stopped if this button is pressed while the appliance is cooking.

* KEEP WARM:

The appliance will automatically switch to Keep Warm mode and begin counting up after pressure cooking, steaming, or slow cooking. The 12-hour duration of Keep Warm. To turn it off, hit the Start/ Stop button or the Keep Warm button.

* Dial:

The accessible functions will light as soon as the Smart Lid Slider is in one of the three positions available. To choose one of the numerous functions, turn the dial.

* Power button:

This button powers on and off the appliance and halts all cooking operations.

HOW TO USE NINJA FOODI SMART LID COOKER

Any packing, stickers and tape should be removed from the appliance and thrown away. To prevent any harm or property damage, pay close attention to operational guidelines, cautions, and critical safety precautions. In warm, soapy water, wash the silicone ring, removable cooking pot, Cook & Crisp Basket, reversible rack, and condensation collector. Rinse, and then completely dry all of the items. Never use a dishwasher to clean the cooker base, a digital cooking probe, or a probe cap. The silicone ring can be put in either direction and is reversible. On the underside of the lid, insert the silicone ring around the outside of the silicone ring rack. Make sure it is put completely and flat beneath the silicone ring rack. When taking food out of the oven, use long-handled tools, protected hot pads, and insulated oven gloves.

* The Condensation Collector's Installation

Slide the condensation collector into the cooker base's slot to install it. After each use, slide it out to remove it for hand washing. After cooking, be sure to remove any extra water that accumulated in the condensation collector.

* *Removal and Installation of The Anticlog Cap*

The anti-clog cap shields users from unwanted food splatters and prevents the valve of the pressure lid from clogging. Each time you use it, you should use a cleaning brush to clean it.
Holding the anti-clog cap between your thumb and bent index finger, turn your wrist in a clockwise direction to remove it. Put it in place and press down to reinstall. Before operating the device, make sure the anti-clog cap is in the proper place. Ensure the silicone ring is securely mounted in the silicone ring rack and the anti-clog cap is securely fastened to the pressure release valve before each usage.

Using The Pressure Function

Move the slider to Pressure. Press the arrow keys to the left of the display to select Hi or LO. The cook time can be changed by using the up and down arrows to the right of the display in minute increments up to 1 hour and then in 5-minute increments from 1 hour to 4 hours. The clock will count down in minutes and seconds if it runs for one hour or less. Only minutes will be counted down if the clock is running for longer than an hour. To start or stop cooking, press Start/Stop. Pressure will start to build in the unit. It will display "PrE" along with a progress bar. When the appliance is fully pressurised, the timer will start to run out.
Depending on the chosen pressure, the time to pressure changes. The cooking pot's current temperatures and the ingredients' temperatures and quantities. When cook time reaches zero, turn the pressure release valve to the VENT position. When the device reads "OPN Lid," it has depressurised, and the lid can be opened by sliding the slider to the right.

Pressure Release Options

After pressure cooking is finished, the appliance offers an automatic and hands-free pressure release setting. If no alternative pressure-release option is used, Natural Release is the default setting for the unit. By holding down the Release Pressure button, you can release pressure at any time. To seal, turn the valve.

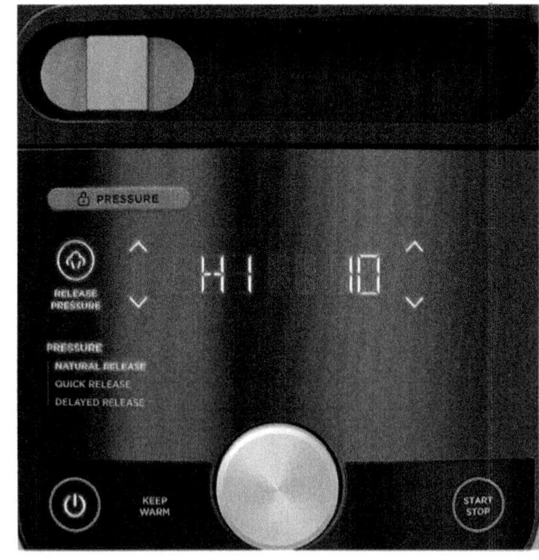

* *Natural Release*

Natural release: When the cooking time is through, the unit will spontaneously depressurise. The meal will continue to cook with the remaining Steam even after the heat is turned off. Any starchy elements, as well as huge or delicate meals, are employed in this.

* *Quick Release*

Smaller meals or ingredients that are susceptible to overcooking are cooked quickly. Never quickly release the pressure while cooking items that are starchy or frothy. Choose this option using the dial to quickly release.

* *Delayed Release*

After the cooking time has passed, set delayed releases for recipes that call for additional time under pressure. If chosen, the time will start at 10 minutes; change it by choosing Release Pressure and then using the up and down arrows. Pressure will then be quickly released by the unit. Particularly effective for rice and other grains

Combi-Steam Mode

Plug the power cord first into a wall outlet before pressing the POWER button to turn the device on. It is not important where the pressure release valve is placed. Either the SEAL or It is possible to position VENT. Ingredients should be added into the pot in accordance with the recipe, either using the Cook & Crisp Basket or the reversible rack. Make sure the pot has enough liquid in it to produce Steam. Put the lid on.
The slider should be set to Combi-Steam mode before selecting Steam Air Fry on the dial. The time and temperature settings will automatically display. Choose a temperature between 150°C and 240°C using the up and down arrow keys to the left of the display. In order to change the cooking time in minute increments up to an hour, use the up and down arrows to the right of the display. To start or stop cooking, press Start/Stop.
"PrE" and progress bars on the LCD indicate that the unit is generating Steam. The number of ingredients in the pot determines how long it will take to Steam. The display will show the set temperature, and the timer will start counting down when the unit reaches the proper steam level. The appliance will beep and display "End" for five minutes when the cooking time reaches zero. Use the up arrows to the right of the display to add more time if your dish needs more time. Preheating is skipped by the device.

* *Steam bake*

Insert the movable rack inside the pot. Ensure there is enough liquid in the pot to create Steam. The base of the Steam Bake should be covered with foil or a baking sheet. The slider is to be set to Combi-Steam mode before selecting Steam Bake using the dial. It will show the current temperature setting. With the up and down arrows to the left of the display, you can select a temperature between 105°C and 210°C in 5°C increments.
The cook time can be changed in one-minute increments up to one hour and fifteen minutes by using the up and down arrows to the right of the display. To start or stop cooking, press Start/Stop. "PrE" and a progress bar showing the unit is creating Steam will be visible on display. It takes 20 minutes to steam. The temperature will be displayed on display, and the timer will start to count down after preheating is finished. The appliance will beep and display "End" for five minutes when the cooking time reaches zero.

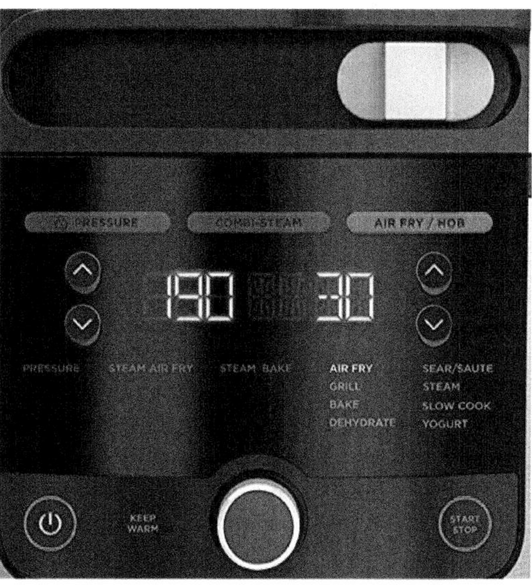

Air Fry/Stove Top Mode

To turn on the Ninja Foodi Smart Lid Cooker, press the POWER button after inserting the power wire into a wall outlet. Pausing the cooking time will result from opening the cover when using Air Fry, Bake, or Grill. Shut the lid to continue.

* *Air fryer*

Either put the Cook & Crisp Basket in the pot or the reversible rack. A diffuser ought to be fastened to the basket. Add ingredients to the reversible rack or Cook & Crisp Basket. Put the lid on. The slider should be set to Air Fry/Hob, then choose Air Fry using the dial. It will show the current temperature setting. Choose a temperature between 150°C and 210°C using arrows for up and down on the left of the display.
In order to change the cooking time in minute increments up to an hour, use the up and down arrows to the right of the display. To start or stop cooking, press Start/Stop. If necessary, you can lift out the basket and open the lid while the food is cooking to shake or toss the ingredients for equal browning. Close the lid after lowering the basket back into the pot. Once the lid is shut, cooking will automatically begin again. The device will beep, and "End" will flash three times on the display when the cooking time reaches zero.

* *Grill*

Either follow the instructions in your recipe or place the reversible rack in the cooker pot in the upper grill position. Arrange the ingredients on the rack, then cover. Slider to Air Fry/Hob, then choose Grill with the dial. Using the Grill function does not require or allow for temperature modification. Up to 30 minutes can be added to the cooking time by using the up and down arrows next to the display. To start or stop cooking, press Start/Stop. The device will flash "End" three times on the display when the cooking time approaches zero.

* *Bake*

Add any additional components and ingredients to the Put the lid on. The slider should be set to Air Fry/Hob, then choose Bake with the dial. It will show the current temperature setting. Choose a temperature between 120°C and 210°C using the arrows to the left of the display. The cook time can be changed by using the up and down arrows to the right of the display in minute increments up to 1 hour and then in 5-minute increments from 1 hour to 4 hours.

To start or stop cooking, press Start/Stop. The device will beep, and "End" will flash three times on the display when the cooking time reaches zero.

* *Dehydrate*

A layer of ingredients should be placed on the reversible rack after it has been lowered into the pot. The slider should be moved to Air Fry/Hob, then select Dehydrate with the dial. It will show the current temperature setting. Between 40°C and 90°C, you can select a temperature using the arrow keys to the left of the display. To change the cooking time from one hour to twelve hours, use the arrow keys on the right side of the display. To start or stop cooking, press Start/Stop. The device will beep, and "End" will flash three times on the display when the cooking time reaches zero.

* *Sear/Sauté*

Add ingredients to the Ninja Foodi cooking pot and move the slider to Air Fry/Hob or remove the cover before choosing Sear/Sauté on the dial. It will show the current temperature setting. To choose "LO 1," "2," "3," "4", or "Hi 5," use the up-and-down arrows to the left of the display. When using the Sear/Sauté feature, there is no time adjustment possible.

To start or stop cooking, press Start/Stop. To switch off the Sear/Sauté feature, press Start/Stop. Press Start/Stop To stop the current cooking function, then use the slider and dial to pick the next function you want to use. Either the lid is open or closed when using this function. When using a cooking pot, always use non-stick utensils. A non-stick coating on the pot will be scratched if metal utensils are used. For "4" and "Hi 5", Sear/Sauté will automatically shut off after 1 hour, and for "Lo 1," "2," and "3," it will do so after 4 hours.

* *Steam*

The Cook & Crisp Basket or reversible rack with the ingredients inside should be placed in the pot after adding 250ml of liquid (or the amount suggested by the recipe). Slider to Air Fry/Hob, then select Steam with the dial. Up to 30 minutes of cook time can be changed by using the arrow keys next to the display. To start or stop cooking, press Start/Stop.

When using the Steam feature, there is no temperature adjustment. In order to get the liquid to boil, the machine will start preheating. "PrE" will appear on the screen. When the appliance achieves temperature, the preheating animation will stop showing, and the timer will start to count down on display. The device will beep, and "End" will flash three times on the display when the cooking time expires.

* *Slow Cook*

The slider should be set to Air Fry/Hob, then select Slow Cook using the dial. It will show the current temperature setting. To choose "Hi," "LO," or "bUFFEt," use the up and down arrows to the left of the display. Up to 12 hours can be added to the cooking time by using the arrow keys on the right side of the display.

To start or stop cooking, press Start/Stop. The Slow Cook Hi time setting can be changed from 4 to 12 hours, while the Slow Cook bUFFEt time setting can be changed from 2 to 12. The appliance will beep, automatically change to Keep Warm, and start counting up once the cooking time hits zero. To turn the Keep Warm option off after cooking is finished, press Keep Warm.

* *Yoghurt*

Add milk to the pot in the desired quantity. Put the lid on. The slider should be set to Air Fry/Hob, then choose yoghurt on the dial. It will show the current temperature setting. To choose "YGt" or "FEr," use the up and down arrows to the left of the display. To change the incubation period between 6 and 12 hours, use the arrow keys on the right side of the display.

To start pasteurization, press Start/Stop. While pasteurizing, the unit will display "boil." The device will emit a beep and indicate "Cool" after the pasteurization temperature has been reached. After the milk has cooled, the device will show Add, Stir, and the incubation time sequentially. Remove the top of the milk and remove the lid. Stir milk and yoghurt cultures together. To start the incubation process, close the lid and press Start Or Stop.

The countdown will start after the device displays "FEr." The device will beep, and the word "End" will flash three times on the display when the incubation period is finished. Until it is turned off, the device will beep once per minute for up to four hours. Before serving, chill yoghurt for up to 12 hours.s

CLEANING AND MAINTENANCE

After each usage, the appliance needs to be completely cleaned. Before cleaning, unplug the device from the electrical socket. Wipe a moist towel over the control panel and cooker base to clean them. Dishwasher-safe components include the cooking pot, silicone ring, reversible rack, Cook & Crisp Basket, and removable diffuser.

The anti-clog cap and pressure release valve can be cleaned with water and dish soap. Fill the cooking pot with water and let it soak before cleaning if food residue is stuck to the cooking pot, reversible rack, or Cook & Crisp Basket. Avoid using scouring pads. If scrubbing is required, use a nylon pad or brush with liquid dish soap or non-abrasive cleaner. After each use, let all pieces air dry.

* *Removing & Reinstalling the Silicone Ring*

Section by section, gently pull the silicone ring outward from the silicone ring rack to remove it. Either side of the ring can be mounted facing upward. Put the silicone ring under the rack with caution to reinstall. Starting with one section, move the silicone ring under the rack gently in both clockwise and anticlockwise directions until you reach the final piece. When placed between two of the metal pins, the final silicone ring part is the simplest to install. Remove any food particles from the silicone ring and anti-clog cap after use.

To prevent odor, keep the silicone ring clean. The smell can be eliminated by washing it in the dishwasher or warm, soapy water. It is, however, typical for it to take in the aroma of some acidic foods. It is advised to keep several silicone rings on hand. Additional silicone rings are available at ninjakitchen.co.uk.

Never use too much force to remove the silicone ring, as this could damage the rack and compromise the pressure-sealing mechanism. Replace any silicone ring that has cracks, cuts, or other damage right away.

How to Clean the Lid?

Prior to using "wet cooking functions," which include Slow Cook, Steam, Sear/Saut é , Pressure, and all Combi-Steam modes, we advise checking the interior of the lid and heating components. We advise Steam cleaning the appliance if you see any food particles or oil buildup, followed by wiping off the interior of the lid.

* Pour 700 ml of water into the pot.
* Move the Smart Lid Slider to the air fryer or stove.
* Choose Steam and give yourself 30 minutes. Press Start/Stop.

Clean the interior of the lid and the heating elements with a moist cloth or sponge once the timer reaches zero, and the gadget has cooled. When cleaning the inside of the lid, stay away from the fan. If required, repeat steps 3 and 4 and spot clean.

CONCLUSION

This Smart Lid Multi-Functional is a blessing for every cook and home chef. Using its 6 liters capacity and the 11 amazing cooking functions, you can create an entire menu for the table. With this beauty resting on your countertop, you won't have to switch from one appliance to another to cook a meal. You can sear/sauté, pressure cook, slow cook, air fry, Bake, broil, dehydrate and steam by moving the slider and pressing a few buttons. So let's just skip the hassle of using multiple appliances and start using Ninja Foodi Smart Lid Cooker from today by trying all the luscious recipes from this cookbook.

CHAPTER 2 BREAKFASTS

BAKED GRAPEFRUIT AND COCONUT

Prep Time: 15 minutes, Cook Time: 15 minutes, Serves: 1

INGREDIENTS:

- 1 grapefruit, halved
- 2 tbsps. desiccated unsweetened coconut

DIRECTIONS:

1. In the Ninja Foodi, add the grapefruit halves. Place 1 tbsp. of coconut on top of each half.
2. Move the slider to Air Fry/Hob, select BAKE. Set the temperature to 180°C and cook until the coconut is browned, about 15 minutes.
3. Transfer the grapefruit halves onto a plate, and use a spoon to eat.

BAKED VANILLA BEAN AND CINNAMON GRANOLA

Prep Time: 5 minutes, Cook Time: 30 minutes, Serves: 3

INGREDIENTS:

- 6 tbsps. coconut oil
- 300 g old-fashioned oats
- 120 ml brown rice syrup
- 2 tsps. vanilla bean powder
- 2 tsps. ground cinnamon
- 50 g Turbindo sugar
- ¼ tsp. sea salt

DIRECTIONS:

1. Use greaseproof paper to line the inner pot.
2. Add all of the ingredients into a large bowl, mix together until well combined with your hands.
3. Form the mixture together into a ball, and place onto Cook & Crisp Basket.
4. Evenly press the mixture on Cook & Crisp Basket, not to break it up into small pieces. This will allow it to bake in large cluster pieces that you can break apart after baking, if you prefer.
5. Move the slider to Air Fry/Hob, select BAKE. Cook at 120°C until crispy, about 30 minutes, not to overbake.
6. After baking, allow to cool completely and serve. As the granola cools, it will harden and get even crispier. Store in an airtight container.

BAKED VANILLA FRUIT GRANOLA

Prep Time: 10 minutes, Cook Time: 15 minutes, Serves: 4

INGREDIENTS:

- 120 g sliced almonds
- 75 g flaxseed
- 70 g flaked unsweetened coconut
- ½ tsp. cinnamon
- ¼ tsp. ginger
- 60 g sultanas
- 1 vanilla bean, split lengthwise and seeds scraped out
- 60 ml coconut oil
- ¼ tsp. nutmeg
- ¼ tsp. sea salt
- 60 g unsweetened dried pineapple chunks

DIRECTIONS:

1. Add all of the ingredients except the dried pineapple chunks to a medium bowl, toss until well combined.
2. Evenly spread the mixture in the pot. Move slider to Air Fry/Hob, select BAKE. Cook at 180°C for 15 minutes, until golden brown, stirring occasionally.
3. Remove from the Ninja Foodi and allow to cool, without stirring.
4. Once cooled, add the pineapple tidbits and stir well.
5. Store in an airtight container.

BANANA BREAKFAST BARS

Prep Time: 10 minutes, Cook Time: 10 minutes, Serves: 2

INGREDIENTS:

* 1 banana
* 65 g spelt flour
* 1/16 tsp. sea salt
* 50 g quinoa flakes
* 1 tbsp. agave nectar

Extra:

* 60 ml grapeseed oil
* 120 ml blackberry jam

DIRECTIONS:

1. In a medium bowl, add the peeled burro bananas and use a fork to mash them.
2. Add the oil and agave nectar to the bowl, stir until well combined, and then stir in the flour, salt, and quinoa flakes until a sticky dough comes together.
3. Use parchment paper to line Cook & Crisp Basket, spread two-third of the prepared dough in its bottom, layer with blackberry jam, and place the remaining dough on the top.
4. Move slider to Air Fry/Hob, select BAKE. Cook at 180°C for 10 minutes and then allow the dough to cool for 15 minutes.
5. Cut the dough into four bars and serve.

CHEESY COURGETTE PANCAKE

Prep Time: 5 minutes, Cook Time: 30 minutes, Serves: 8

INGREDIENTS:

* 135 g plain flour
* 2 tsps. baking powder
* ½ tsp. salt
* 2 tbsps. rapeseed or sunflower oil, plus more for greasing
* 120 g cheese
* 1 small grated courgette
* 250 ml plant-based milk
* 1½ tsps. vanilla extract
* 1 tbsp. agave, brown sugar, or maple syrup
* ¼ tsp. lemon zest
* ½ tbsp. ground flaxseed added in step 2
* Vegan butter
* Maple syrup or maple agave syrup

DIRECTIONS:

1. Lightly grease the inner pot.
2. Combine all the ingredients in a medium bowl. Gently toss until the batter is smooth, but there's no need to remove all the lumps.
3. Move slider to Air Fry/Hob, select BAKE. Cook at 200ºC. Scoop out the batter and pour into the Ninja Foodi. Once bubbles begin to form in the centre of the pancake, turn the pancake over to cook the other side until light brown. Remove from the pot and repeat with the remaining batter.

EASY BAKED CHICKPEA FALAFEL

Prep Time: 15 minutes, plus overnight, Cook Time: 30 minutes, Serves: 6

INGREDIENTS:

* 200 g dried chickpeas
* 20 g chopped fresh coriander (or parsley if preferred)
* ½ chopped yellow onion
* 20 g chopped fresh parsley
* 3 garlic cloves, peeled1½ tbsps. chickpea flour or wheat flour (if gluten is not a concern)
* 1 tsp. ground coriander
* ½ tsp. baking powder
* 2 tsps. ground cumin
* 2 tbsps. freshly squeezed lemon juice

DIRECTIONS:

1. The night before making falafel, add the dried chickpeas in a large bowl, pour in the water to cover by 7 cm. Cover the bowl and allow to soak for at least 8 hours or overnight. Drain.
2. Use greaseproof paper to line the inner pot.
3. Combine the soaked chickpeas and the remaining ingredients in a high-speed blender or food processor. Blend until all ingredients are well combined but not smooth, it should have the consistency of sand but stick together when pressed.
4. Divide the falafel mixture into 20 balls with a biscuit scoop or two spoons and place them in the inner pot. Lightly flatten each ball using the bottom of a measuring cup. This will help them cook more evenly.
5. Move slider to Air Fry/Hob, select BAKE. Cook at 190°C for 15 minutes. Flip and bake for another 10 to 15 minutes, until lightly browned.
6. Place in an airtight container and refrigerate for up to 1 week or freeze for up to 1 month.

HEALTHY COURGETTE BAKED EGGS

Prep Time: 10 minutes, Cook Time: 1 hour, Serves: 6

INGREDIENTS:

* 1 medium courgette, shredded
* 230 g Spinach leaves
* 230 g Eggs
* 250 ml half-and-half
* 1 tbsp. Olive oil
* 1 tsp. Sea salt
* 1 tsp. Black pepper
* 350 g Shredded mozzarella cheese
* 60 g Feta cheese
* 2 cloves Garlic, crushed and peeled
* Olive oil spray

DIRECTIONS:

1. Grease the inner pot with olive oil spray. Set aside.
2. Add the olive oil to a non-stick pan. Set the pan on a medium flame and heat.
3. Once done, whisk in the garlic, spinach, and courgette. Cook for about 5 minutes. Set aside.
4. Add the half-and-half, eggs, pepper, and salt to a large mixing bowl. Toss well to combine.
5. Whisk in the feta cheese and shredded mozzarella cheese (reserve 30 g of mozzarella cheese for later).
6. Pour the egg mixture and prepared spinach to the inner pot. Toss well to combine. Top with the reserved cheese. Move slider to Air Fry/Hob, select BAKE. Cook the egg mixture at 190ºC for about 45 minutes.
7. Let rest for 10 minutes. Slice and serve!

HERBED BREAKFAST BEAN SAUSAGE

Prep Time: 20 minutes, Cook Time: 30 minutes, Serves: 4

INGREDIENTS:

* 1 small onion, cut into quarters
* 2 garlic cloves
* 1 carrot, peeled and cut into large chunks
* ½ tsp. fennel seeds
* Water, as needed
* 400 g tinned pinto beans, drained
* 1 tbsp. nutritional yeast
* 1 tbsp. ground almonds or almond meal
* ½ tsp. dried oregano (1 tsp. fresh)
* 1 tsp. smoked paprika
* ½ tsp. dried thyme (1 tsp. fresh)
* ½ tsp. dried sage (1 tsp. fresh)
* ½ tsp. dried basil (1 tsp. fresh)
* ½ tsp. sea salt

DIRECTIONS:

1. Use a silicone mat or greaseproof paper to line the inner pot.
2. Add the onion, garlic, and carrot in a food processor. Chop until fine, or use hand to chop.
3. Add the onion-carrot mixture, and the fennel seeds into the Ninja Foodi. Move slider to Air Fry/Hob, then select Sear/Sauté and cook at 200ºC for about 4 minutes or until the vegetables are soft, adding water if needed. Remove from the heat and allow to cool.
4. Add the pinto beans to the food processor, pulse until roughly chopped, but not to a paste. Add the onion-carrot mixture to the processor, and process until blended.
5. Pour the contents into a medium bowl. Add the yeast, ground almond, oregano, paprika, thyme, sage, basil, and salt. Mix until combined.
6. Measure 4 tbsps. of sausage and use your hand to shape into a patty. Then place each patty into the inner pot carefully. Continue with the remaining sausage.
7. Move slider to Air Fry/Hob, select BAKE. Cook at 205°C for 25 to 30 minutes, until crispy on the outside but still moist on the inside.
8. After baking, remove from the pot and allow to cool for a few minutes and serve.

JAMAICAN JERK VEGETABLE PATTIES

Prep Time: 20 minutes, Cook Time: 1 hour, Serves: 3-4

INGREDIENTS:

Filling:

* 70 g diced green pepper
* 200 g cooked chickpeas
* 200 g chopped pumpkin
* ½ of a diced onions
* 200 g chopped mushrooms
* 1 tbsp. of onion powder
* 1 tsp. of ginger
* 2 tsps. of thyme
* 1 tbsp. of agave syrup
* ½ tsp. of cayenne powder
* 1 tsp. of allspice
* ¼ tsp. of cloves
* 1 tsp. of pure sea salt
* 1 chopped plum tomato

Crust:

* 1 tbsp. of grapeseed oil
* 200 g of spelt flour
* 1 tsp. of pure sea salt
* ⅛ tsp. of ginger powder
* 1 tsp. of onion powder
* 250 ml of spring water
* 60 ml of aquafaba

DIRECTIONS:

1. In a food processor, add all of the vegetables, except the plum tomatoes. Pulse a few times to chop them into large pieces.
2. In a large bowl, combine the blended vegetables with seasonings and tomatoes. This constitutes the filling for the patties.
3. Add the grapeseed oil, spelt flour, pure sea salt, ginger powder and onion powder in a separate large bowl, mix well.
4. Pour in 120 ml of spring water and knead the dough into a ball, adding more water or flour as needed.
5. Allow the dough to rest for 5 to 10 minutes. Knead again for a few minutes then evenly divide it into 8 portions.
6. Make each portion into a ball and roll each ball out into a 17-cm circle.
7. Take a dough circle and place 120 ml of the filling in the centre. Use the aquafaba to brush all edges of the dough, fold it in half and use a fork to seal the edges together.
8. Repeat step 8 until all the dough circles are filled.
9. Use a little grapeseed oil to lightly coat the inner pot.
10. Move slider to Air Fry/Hob, select BAKE. Cook filled patties at 180°C for about 25 to 30 minutes until golden brown.
11. Serve warm.

MAPLE OAT COCONUT FLAX GRANOLA

Prep Time: 15 minutes, Cook Time: 30 to 45 minutes, Serves: 6

INGREDIENTS:

* 2 tbsps. avocado oil
* 2 tbsps. finely shredded unsweetened coconut
* 2 tbsps. ground almonds
* 2 tbsps. flax meal
* 2 tbsps. maple syrup, or 5 to 6 small dates, pitted
* ¼ tsp. vanilla extract
* 2 tbsps. brown rice flour
* Pinch sea salt
* 75 g rolled oats

DIRECTIONS:

1. Combine the oil, coconut, ground almonds, flax meal, and maple syrup in a food processor, process until smooth.
2. Pour the mixture into a bowl and stir in the vanilla, flour, and salt. Stir in the oats.
3. Evenly spread the mixture in the pot. Move slider to Air Fry/Hob, select BAKE. Cook at 180°C for 30 to 45 minutes, turning every 15 minutes, until golden brown. After baking, allow to cool. Store in an airtight container.

MARGHERITA PIZZA WITH VEGGIES

Prep Time: 25 minutes, Cook Time: 1 hour, Serves: 4

INGREDIENTS:

Crust:

* 200 g spelt flour
* ½ tsp. of basil
* ½ tsp. of pure sea salt
* ½ tsp. of onion powder
* ½ tsp. of oregano
* 250 ml of spring water

Cheese:

* 1 tsp. of sea mossgel
* 120 g of soaked Brazil nuts (overnight or for at least 3 hours)
* ½ tsp. of oregano
* ½ tsp. of basil
* ¼ tsp. of pure sea salt
* ½ tsp. of onion powder
* 60 ml of homemade hempseed milk
* 1 tsp. of key lime juice
* 120 ml of spring water

Toppings:

* "garlic" sauce
* sliced red onions
* sliced plum or cherry tomatoes
* chopped fresh basil

DIRECTIONS:

1. Add the spelt flour and seasonings in a medium bowl, and mix well. Pour in 120 ml of spring water and mix. Continue to add more water until the dough can be formed into a ball.
2. Spread the flour on your working surface. Use a rolling pin to roll the dough out, adding more flour as necessary to avoid sticking.
3. Spread the dough out on Cook & Crisp Basket, use the grapeseed oil to brush, and use a fork to make holes. Place in the Ninja Foodi. Move slider to Air Fry/Hob, select BAKE and cook at 180°C 10 to 15 minutes.
4. In a blender, add all of the ingredients for the cheese. Blend well until consistency is smooth.
5. Take the dough out from the cooker. Spread with "garlic" sauce and prepared cheese. Place the onions, sliced tomatoes, basil, and more cheese on the top of the pizza.
6. Bake for 10 to 15 minutes at 220°C.
7. Serve warm.

BAKED EGG AND AVOCADO

Prep Time: 5 minutes, Cook Time: 15 minutes, Serves: 2

INGREDIENTS:

* 1 large ripe avocado
* 2 large eggs
* 4 tbsps. jarred pesto, for serving
* 2 tbsps. chopped tomato, for serving
* 2 tbsps. crumbled feta, for serving (optional)
* Salt
* Freshly ground black pepper

DIRECTIONS:

1. Cut the avocado in half and remove the core. Scoop out 1 to 2 tbsps. from each half to create a hole large enough to fit an egg. Put the avocado halves in the inner pot, cut-side up.
2. Crack 1 egg in each avocado half and season with salt and pepper.
3. Move slider to Air Fry/Hob, select BAKE and cook at 220ºC 10 to 15 minutes until the eggs are set and cooked to the desired doneness.
4. Transfer to a bowl and top each avocado with pesto, chopped tomato, and crumbled feta.

OATMEAL STUFFED APPLE CRUMBLE

Prep Time: 5 minutes, Cook Time: 20 to 25 minutes, Serves: 4

INGREDIENTS:

* 4 small apples
* 50 g gluten-free rolled oats
* 3 or 4 small dates, pitted
* 18 g unsweetened shredded coconut
* 1 tsp. maple syrup
* ⅛ tsp. ground cinnamon
* 1 tsp. coconut oil
* ⅛ tsp. vanilla extract
* ⅛ tsp. sea salt

DIRECTIONS:

1. Core each apple, but leave the bottom intact to form a cup. Place each apple on a 20-cm square of aluminium foil.
2. Combine the oats and the remaining ingredients in a high-speed blender or food processor, blend until well combined.
3. Fill 2 tbsps. of the oat mixture into each apple.
4. Wrap the foil around each apple, leaving a bit of the top exposed, and arrange the apples on a Cook & Crisp Basket. Move slider to Air Fry/Hob, select BAKE and cook at 205°C until the apples are tender and the filling is golden, about 20 to 25 minutes.

RAINBOW VEGETABLE BREAKFAST HASH

Prep Time: 15 minutes, Cook Time: 25 minutes, Serves: 4

INGREDIENTS:

* 2 rosemary sprigs, leaves removed and minced
* 1 tbsp. dried thyme
* 1 tsp. Hungarian paprika
* ½ tsp. freshly ground black pepper
* 2 parsnips, cut into 1-cm cubes
* 2 large sweet potatoes, cut into 1-cm cubes
* 2 Waxy potatoes, cut into 1-cm cubes
* 1 rutabaga, cut into 1-cm cubes
* 4 large carrots, cut into 1-cm cubes
* 3 garlic cloves, minced
* 1 large onion, diced
* 400 g can chickpeas, drained and rinsed
* 400 g can red kidney beans, drained and rinsed

DIRECTIONS:

1. Use greaseproof paper to line the inner pot.
2. Add the rosemary, thyme, paprika, and pepper in a small bowl, stir well and set aside.
3. Fill the water in a large pot, bring to a boil over high heat. Add the parsnips, sweet potatoes, Waxy potatoes, rutabaga and carrots. Parboil for 2 minutes. Drain well but don't rinse. Place them into a large bowl. Toss in the thyme mixture and coat well. Spread the parboiled vegetables in the inner pot and sprinkle with the garlic and onion.
4. Move slider to Air Fry/Hob, select BAKE and cook at 190°C until the vegetables are fork-tender, about 20 minutes.
5. Stir together the chickpeas and kidney beans in a medium bowl. Serve with the cooked vegetable hash.

SPELT BANANA WALNUT BREAD

Prep Time: 10 minutes, Cook Time: 20 minutes, Serves: 2

INGREDIENTS:

* 400 g banana
* 60 ml agave syrup
* 1⅓ tbsps. olive oil
* 100 g spelt flour
* 40 g chopped walnuts
* ⅛ tsp. salt

DIRECTIONS:

1. In a medium bowl, add the banana, use a fork to mash it and stir in the agave syrup and oil until combined.
2. Place the flour in a separate medium bowl, add the nuts and salt, stir until mixed, and then stir in the burro banana mixture until smooth.
3. Pour the batter into the Ninja Foodi pot. Move slider to Air Fry/Hob, select BAKE and cook at 180°C for 20 minutes until firm and the top turn golden brown.
4. After baking, allow the bread to cool for 10 minutes, then cut into slices and serve.

CHAPTER 3 STARTER AND SALAD

QUICK CRISPS

Prep Time: 10 minutes, Cook Time: 1 hour, plus 30 minutes to cool, Serves: 6

INGREDIENTS:

* 1 kg medium white potatoes
* 1 to 2 tbsps. unsalted seasoning

DIRECTIONS:

1. Use greaseproof paper to line the inner pot.
2. Wash and scrub the potatoes, and put them on Cook & Crisp Basket. Move slider to Air Fry/Hob, select BAKE and cook at 205°C for 45 minutes, or until easily pierced with a fork. Remove and set aside, clean the inner pot.
3. Take the potatoes out from the pot, let cool in the refrigerator for about 30 minutes, or until you're ready to make a batch of chips.
4. Select BAKE and preheat the pot to 220°C. Use greaseproof paper to line the pot.
5. Slice the cooled potatoes into slices, then place them in a large bowl, add the unsalted seasoning and toss well.
6. On Cook & Crisp Basket, spread with the coated slices in an even layer. Select BAKE and cook for about 7 minutes, then take them out from the inner pot, flip the chips over, and redistribute them in an even layer. Bake for an additional 8 minutes, or until the potatoes are crisp and golden brown. Then serve.

VANILLA SPICED QUINOA PUMPKIN BAKE

Prep Time: 15 minutes, Cook Time: 15 minutes, Serves: 6

INGREDIENTS:

* Cooking spray
* 600 g cooked quinoa
* 1 vanilla bean, split lengthwise and seeds scraped out
* 400 g can pumpkin purée
* 120 ml water
* ½ tsp. nutmeg
* ½ tsp. ground ginger
* 1 tsp. cinnamon
* ¼ tsp. grated fresh ginger
* ¼ tsp. sea salt

DIRECTIONS:

1. Spray a 1-L baking dish with cooking spray and set aside.
2. Add the quinoa and the remaining ingredients in a medium bowl, stir them together.
3. Place the mixture into the Ninja Foodi. Move slider to Air Fry/Hob, select BAKE. Cook at 180°C for 15 minutes, or until golden and bubbly.

NUTTY SPINACH, ARTICHOKE AND TOMATO DIP

Prep Time: 10 minutes, Cook Time: 20 minutes, Serves: 6

INGREDIENTS:

* Cooking spray
* 180 ml unsweetened almond milk
* 1 garlic clove
* 90 g raw cashews
* 2 tbsps. freshly squeezed lemon juice
* ¾ tsp. sea salt
* 1 tbsp. nutritional yeast
* 150 g baby spinach leaves
* 120 g baby tomatoes
* 150 g artichoke hearts, frozen or canned in water, not oil

DIRECTIONS:

1. Use cooking spray to coat the inner pot.
2. Add the almond milk, garlic, cashews, lemon juice, salt and yeast into a blender. Blend until very smooth.
3. Add the spinach, tomatoes and artichoke hearts to the blender. Pulse to combine, but still leaving chunks of vegetables.
4. Place the dip into the pot. Move slider to Air Fry/Hob, select BAKE and cook at 220°C for 20 minutes.
5. After baking, remove from the inner pot, allow to cool for 5 minutes, and serve warm.

SPICED PARTY MIX

Prep Time: 15 minutes, Cook Time: 10 minutes, Serves: 6

INGREDIENTS:

* Cooking spray
* 35 g unsweetened coconut flakes
* 120 g sultanas
* 120 g raw almonds
* 60 g roasted peas
* 70 g pumpkin seeds
* 150 g dried pineapple pieces
* 1 tsp. chilli powder
* 1 tsp. ground ginger
* 2 tbsps. garlic powder
* 2 tbsps. onion powder
* 1 tsp. sea salt
* 1 tbsp. coconut oil

DIRECTIONS:

1. Use cooking spray to coat the pot.
2. Combine all of the remaining ingredients in a medium bowl.
3. In the Ninja Foodi, spread the mixture in an even layer.
4. Move slider to Air Fry/Hob, select BAKE. Cook at 220°C for 10 minutes, being careful that it doesn't burn.
5. After baking, remove from the inner pot and allow to cool before serving.

SWEET POTATO SALAD WITH SPICY CASHEW CORIANDER DRESSING

Prep Time: 10 minutes, Cook Time: 25 minutes, Serves: 1 or 2

INGREDIENTS:

For The Sweet Potatoes:

* 2 tbsps. avocado oil
* 3 medium sweet potatoes, peeled and cubed
* 1 tsp. ground paprika
* 2 garlic cloves, crushed
* ½ tsp. sea salt

For The Jalapeño-Coriander Dressing:

* 120 g raw cashews
* ½ to 1 jalapeño
* 240 ml water
* 10 g fresh coriander leaves
* 2 tbsps. freshly squeezed lime juice
* ½ tsp. sea salt

For Assembling:

* 60 g mixed salad greens

DIRECTIONS:

1. Use greaseproof paper to line the inner pot.

TO PREPARE THE SWEET POTATOES:

1. Combine the avocado oil, potatoes, paprika, garlic and salt in a medium bowl, toss them together.
2. Evenly spread the sweet potato cubes in the Ninja Foodi. Move slider to Air Fry/Hob, select BAKE. Cook at 180°C for 25 minutes.

TO PREPARE THE JALAPEÑO-CORIANDER DRESSING:

1. While the sweet potatoes bake, add the cashews, jalapeño, water, coriander, lime juice and salt into a high-speed blender, blend them together until smooth.

TO ASSEMBLE:

1. On 1 large or 2 small plates, add the mixed salad greens. Place the warm sweet potatoes on the top, drizzle with the dressing, and enjoy.

BARLEY SALAD WITH LEMON-TAHINI SAUCE

Prep Time: 15 minutes, Cook Time: 45 minutes, Serves: 4 to 6

INGREDIENTS:

* 300 g pearl barley
* 5 tbsps. extra-virgin olive oil, divided
* 1½ tsps. coarse salt, for cooking barley
* 60 ml tahini
* 1 tsp. grated lemon zest plus (60 ml) juice (2 lemons)
* 1 tbsp. sumac, divided
* 1 garlic clove, minced
* 4 spring onions, sliced thin
* ¾ tsp. coarse salt
* 1 English cucumber, cut into 1-cm pieces
* 1 red pepper, stemmed, seeded, and chopped
* 1 carrot, peeled and shredded
* 2 tbsps. finely chopped jarred hot cherry peppers
* 10 g coarsely chopped fresh mint

DIRECTIONS:

1. Mix 1½ L water, 1 tbsp. oil, barley, and 1½ tsps. salt in Ninja Foodi pot.
2. Move the slider to PRESSURE. Close the lid, then turn the pressure release valve to SEAL position. Cook for 8 minutes. Turn off and let pressure release naturally for 15 minutes. Quick-release any remaining pressure, then carefully remove lid, letting steam escape away from you. Drain barley, spread onto rimmed baking sheet, and let cool for about 15 minutes.
3. Meanwhile, whisk remaining 60 ml oil, 1 tsp. sumac, 2 tbsps. water, tahini, lemon zest and juice, garlic, and ¾ tsp. salt in a large bowl until well mixed, set aside for 15 minutes.
4. Measure out and reserve 120 ml dressing for serving. Add barley, carrot, spring onions, cucumber, red pepper, and cherry peppers to bowl with dressing and gently toss. Season with salt and pepper. Transfer salad to a dish and sprinkle with mint and remaining sumac. Serve with reserved dressing separately.

CRANBERRIES, ALMONDS AND WILD RICE SALAD

Prep Time: 10 minutes, Cook Time: 36 minutes, Serves: 18

INGREDIENTS:

For The Rice:

* 600 ml Vegetable Broth or Chicken Bone Broth
* 400 g wild rice blend, rinsed
* 1 tsp. coarse salt

For The Dressing:

* 60 ml extra-virgin olive oil
* 60 ml white wine vinegar
* Juice of 1 medium orange (about 60 ml)
* 1 tsp. honey or pure maple syrup
* 1½ tsp. grated orange zest

For The Salad:

* Freshly ground black pepper
* 90 g unsweetened dried cranberries
* 60 g sliced almonds, toasted

DIRECTIONS:

TO MAKE THE RICE:

1. Combine the rice, salt, and broth in the Ninja pressure cooker.
2. Move the slider to PRESSURE. Close the lid, then turn the pressure release valve to SEAL position. Cook for 25 minutes.
3. Once cooking is complete, press Stop and allow the pressure to release naturally for 15 minutes, then quick release any remaining pressure.
4. When the pin drops, unlock and remove the lid.
5. Let the rice cool slightly, then fluff it with a fork.

TO MAKE THE DRESSING:

1. In a small jar with a screw-top lid, mix the olive oil, zest, juice, vinegar, and honey. Shake to combine.

TO MAKE THE SALAD:

1. Combine the rice, almonds and cranberries in a large bowl.
2. Add the dressing and season with pepper.
3. Serve immediately or refrigerated.

FARRO AND STRAWBERRY SALAD

Prep Time: 17 minutes, Cook Time: 18 minutes, Serves: 8

INGREDIENTS:

For the farro:

* 200 g farro, rinsed and drained
* ¼ tsp. coarse salt

For the salad:

* 85 g sliced strawberries
* 30 g sliced almonds, toasted
* Fresh basil leaves, cut into a chiffonade, for garnish
* Freshly ground black pepper

For the dressing:

* ½ tbsp. fruit-flavoured balsamic vinegar
* 1 tbsp. freshly squeezed lime juice (from ½ medium lime)
* ½ tsp. Dijon mustard
* ½ tsp. poppy seeds
* ½ tbsp. honey or pure maple syrup
* 60 ml extra-virgin olive oil

DIRECTIONS:

TO MAKE THE FARRO:

1. Combine the farro, salt, and 500 ml of water in the electric pressure cooker.
2. Move the slider to PRESSURE. Close the lid, then turn the pressure release valve to SEAL position. Cook for 10 minutes.
3. Once cooking is complete, allow the pressure to Ninja naturally for 10 minutes, then quick release the remaining pressure. Press Stop.
4. When the pin drops, unlock and remove the lid.
5. Fluff the farro with a fork and cool it down.

TO MAKE THE DRESSING:

1. In a small jar with a screw-top lid, combine the balsamic vinegar, lime juice, mustard, poppy seeds, honey, and olive oil. Shake until well combined.

TO MAKE THE SALAD:

1. Toss the farro with the dressing in a large bowl. Stir in the strawberries and almonds.
2. Serve seasoned with pepper, and garnished with basil.

LEMONY BLACK RICE AND EDAMAME SALAD

Prep Time: 15 minutes, Cook Time: 28 minutes, Serves: 8

INGREDIENTS:

For the rice:

* 200 g black rice, rinsed and kept wet

For the dressing:

* 3 tbsps. extra-virgin olive oil
* 2 tbsps. freshly squeezed lemon juice
* 2 tbsps. rice vinegar
* 1 tbsp. honey or pure maple syrup
* 1 tbsp. sesame oil

For the salad:

* 225 g frozen shelled edamame, thawed
* 30 g chopped walnuts
* 2 spring onions, both white and green parts, thinly sliced
* coarse salt
* Freshly ground black pepper

DIRECTIONS:

TO MAKE THE FARRO:

1. Combine the farro, salt, and 500 ml of water in the electric pressure cooker.
2. Move the slider to PRESSURE. Close the lid, then turn the pressure release valve to SEAL position. Cook for 10 minutes.
3. Once cooking is complete, allow the pressure to Ninja naturally for 10 minutes, then quick release the remaining pressure. Press Stop.
4. When the pin drops, unlock and remove the lid.
5. Fluff the farro with a fork and cool it down.

TO MAKE THE DRESSING:

1. In a small jar with a screw-top lid, combine the balsamic vinegar, lime juice, mustard, poppy seeds, honey, and olive oil. Shake until well combined.

TO MAKE THE SALAD:

1. Toss the farro with the dressing in a large bowl. Stir in the strawberries and almonds.
2. Serve seasoned with pepper, and garnished with basil.

WHITE BEAN CUCUMBER SALAD

Prep Time: 10 minutes, Cook Time: 20 minutes, Serves: 4

INGREDIENTS:

* 1 tbsp. plus 1 tsp. coarse salt (or 2 tsps. fine salt), divided
* 400 g dried cannellini beans
* 4 tbsps. plus 1 tsp. extra-virgin olive oil, divided
* 1-litre water
* 3 tbsps. freshly squeezed lemon juice
* ¼ tsp. freshly ground black pepper
* 1 tsp. ground cumin
* 1 large celery stalk, chopped
* 1 medium red or green pepper, chopped
* 1 large tomato, seeded and chopped
* ½ cucumber, peeled, seeded, and chopped
* 3 or 4 spring onions, chopped
* 120 g crumbled feta cheese (optional)
* 10 g minced fresh parsley
* 2 tbsps. minced fresh mint

DIRECTIONS:

1. Dissolve 1 tbsp. of coarse salt (or 1½ tsps. of fine salt) in 1 litre of water in a large bowl. Add the beans and let them soak at room temperature for 8 to 24 hours.
2. Drain and rinse the beans. Transfer them into the Foodi pot. Add 1 tsp. of olive oil and stir to coat the beans. Add ½ tsp. of coarse salt (or ¼ tsp. of fine salt) and 1 litre of water.
3. Move the slider to PRESSURE. Close the lid, then turn the pressure release valve to SEAL position. Cook time to 5 minutes. Press Start/Stop to begin.
4. Meanwhile, combine 3 tbsps. of olive oil and the lemon juice and in a small jar with a tight-fitting lid. Add the remaining ½ tsp. of coarse salt (or ¼ tsp. of fine salt), the pepper and cumin. Cover the jar and shake the spices until thoroughly combined.
5. When the cooking is complete, naturally release the pressure for 10 minutes, then quick release any remaining pressure. Unlock and remove the Pressure Lid carefully.
6. Drain the beans and place them into a bowl. Immediately pour the dressing over the beans and toss to coat. Allow to cool to room temperature, stirring occasionally.
7. Add the celery, pepper, tomato, cucumber, spring onions, and feta cheese (if using, omit for a dairy-free and vegan dish) to the beans. Gently toss well. Add the parsley and mint, toss to combine before serving.

CHAPTER 4 VEGETABLE AND MEATLESS

CHEESY SCALLOP POTATO AND ONION

Prep Time: 10 minutes, Cook Time: 45 minutes, Serves: 4

INGREDIENTS:

* 1 tbsp. avocado oil
* 1½ onions, diced into small pieces
* 8 small new potatoes, thinly sliced
* 1 tbsp. chopped fresh tarragon
* 1 tsp. freshly ground black pepper
* 1 tsp. sea salt
* 1 recipe cashew cheese sauce

DIRECTIONS:

1. Add the avocado oil, onions and potatoes into the inner pot, mix to coat well. Add the tarragon, pepper and salt, toss again. Take it out and set aside, clean the inner pot.
2. Layer the potatoes in 3 rows in Cook & Crisp Basket. Overlap and stand them up as necessary to fit in the dish. Sprinkle the diced onions between the potato slices and rows.
3. Move slider to Air Fry/Hob, select BAKE and cook at 180°C for about 45 minutes, or until the potatoes are tender.
4. After baking, remove from the inner pot, and top the potatoes with the cheese sauce. Transfer to 4 plates and enjoy immediately, or place the dish back to the Ninja Foodi to heat the sauce for 5 minutes before serving.

EASY BAKED SWEET POTATO AND APPLE

Prep Time: 5 minutes, Cook Time: 40 minutes, Serves: 1

INGREDIENTS:

* 1 medium sweet potato
* 1 medium apple, peeled and diced
* Pinch sea salt
* ½ tsp. cinnamon

DIRECTIONS:

1. Cut lengthwise of the sweet potato, about 2½ cm deep. Spread the potato open and put it in a baking dish.
2. Inside the sweet potato's opening, add the apple. Sprinkle the salt and cinnamon over the top.
3. Put the dish in the Ninja Foodi. Move slider to Air Fry/Hob, select BAKE. Cover the lid and cook at 180°C for 40 minutes, or until the potato is tender.
4. After baking, allow to cool slightly and serve warm.

GARLIC PEPPER-STUFFED PORTOBELLO MUSHROOMS

Prep Time: 10 minutes, Cook Time: 20 minutes, Serves: 2

INGREDIENTS:

For The Mushrooms:

* 2 large portobello mushrooms
* Avocado oil, for rubbing
* Freshly ground black pepper
* Sea salt

For The Stuffing:

* 2 tsps. avocado oil
* 2 garlic cloves, crushed
* ½ red pepper, diced
* ½ orange pepper, diced
* ½ yellow pepper, diced
* ¼ diced red onion
* ½ tsp. sea salt
* ½ tsp. freshly ground black pepper

DIRECTIONS:

1. Use greaseproof paper to line the inner pot.

TO PREPARE THE MUSHROOMS:

1. Quickly rinse and dry the mushrooms. Remove the stems, and scoop out the black gills with the tip pf a spoon. Rub the avocado oil all over of the mushrooms, and sprinkle with pepper and salt.
2. Transfer the mushrooms to the pot. Move slider to Air Fry/Hob, select BAKE and cook at 180°C for 15 to 20 minutes.

TO PREPARE THE STUFFING:

1. While the mushrooms are baking, stir together the avocado oil, garlic, peppers, onion, salt, and pepper in a small bowl until well combined.

TO ASSEMBLE:

1. After baking, remove the mushrooms from the inner pot, and discard any accumulated liquid.
2. Evenly divide the stuffing mixture between the 2 mushrooms and serve immediately.

MASHED SWEET POTATO

Prep Time: 15 minutes, Cook Time: 30 minutes, Serves: 6

INGREDIENTS:

* 8 sweet potatoes, cooked
* 1 tbsp. dried sage
* 120 ml vegetable broth
* 1 tsp. dried thyme
* 1 tsp. dried rosemary

DIRECTIONS:

1. Remove and discard the skin from the cooked sweet potatoes, place them in the inner pot. Use a fork or potato masher to mash the sweet potatoes, then stir in the remaining ingredients.
2. Remove and discard the skin from the cooked sweet potatoes, place them in the inner pot. Use a fork or potato masher to mash the sweet potatoes, then stir in the remaining ingredients.
3. Move slider to Air Fry/Hob, select BAKE and cook at 190°C for 30 minutes, after baking, serve warm.

ROASTED COURGETTE LASAGNE

Prep Time: 10 minutes, Cook Time: 25 minutes, Serves: 2

INGREDIENTS:

* 4 courgettes, sliced lengthwise into ½-cm noodles
* 250 ml sun-dried tomato sauce
* 250 ml white sauce

DIRECTIONS:

1. In the inner pot, add the courgette noodles. press Roast and cook at 180°C for 10 minutes, then remove from the Ninja Foodi.
2. Cover the bottom with one layer of courgette strips in the inner pot. Pour 60 ml sun-dried tomato sauce over. Then add another layer of courgette strip, placed
3. crosswise from the first layer. Cover with another 60 ml sun-dried tomato sauce.Lay a third layer of courgette crosswise from the second layer and another 60 mlsun-dried tomato sauce. Repeat with the remaining courgette and 60 ml sun-dried tomato sauce.
4. Place the white sauce on top of the finished lasagne. Move slider to Air Fry/Hob, select BAKE. Cover the lid, and bake for 15 minutes, or until hot and bubbly.
5. Remove from the Ninja Foodi and allow to cool for 5 minutes before slicing and serving.

SPICED COURGETTE DISH

Prep Time: 10 minutes, Cook Time: 20 minutes, Serves: 2

INGREDIENTS:

* 1 tbsp. onion powder
* 2 tbsps. agave syrup
* 1 tsp. liquid smoke
* 1 tbsp. of sea salt
* ½ tsp. cayenne powder
* 50 g date sugar
* 60 ml spring water
* 2 courgettes, cut into strips
* 1 tbsp. rapeseed oil

DIRECTIONS:

1. Place a medium saucepan over medium heat, add all of the ingredients except for the courgette and oil, cook until the sugar has dissolved.
2. In a large bowl, add the courgette strips, pour in the mixture from the saucepan, toss until coated, and allow it to marinate for at least 1 hour.
3. When ready to cook, switch on the Ninja Foodi.
4. Use the greaseproof paper to line the inner pot, grease with the oil, arrange the marinated courgette strips on it. Move slider to Air Fry/Hob, select BAKE and cook at 205°C for 10 minutes.
5. Then flip the courgette over, continue to cook for 4 minutes and then allow to cool completely.
6. Serve immediately.

STUFFED SWEET POTATO WITH BROCCOLI-ALMOND PESTO

Prep Time: 10 minutes, Cook Time: 1½ hours, Serves: 2

INGREDIENTS:

* 2 large sweet potatoes
* 2 tbsps. avocado oil
* 175 g broccoli
* 300 g almonds
* 2 garlic cloves
* 20 g fresh basil leaves
* ¼ an onion
* 40 g nutritional yeast
* ½ tsp. sea salt

DIRECTIONS:

1. Use a fork to pierce the sweet potatoes all over. Add the sweet potatoes into the pot. Move slider to Air Fry/Hob, select BAKE and cook at 180°C for 1 hour and 15 minutes, or until they are soft.
2. While the sweet potatoes are baking, prepare the pesto. Combine the remaining ingredients in a food processor, pulse until the broccoli and almonds are ground into small pieces. Adjust the seasonings, if needed.
3. When the potatoes are ready, cut them in half lengthwise, and scoop out the insides of the potato gently, not to tear the potato skin, add the baked potato filling to a medium bowl, then add the pesto mixture, stir together gently.
4. Divide the mixture in half, fill each half into the two empty potato skins, and serve.

TEMPEH ONION STUFFED CREMINI MUSHROOMS

Prep Time: 15 minutes, Cook Time: 20 minutes, Serves: 6

INGREDIENTS:

* 18 cremini mushrooms
* 2 tbsps. diced red onion, cut into small dice
* 85 g tempeh, cut into very small dice
* Pinch of cayenne pepper
* Pinch of onion powder
* 50 g rice, cooked
* 1 tbsp. tamari

DIRECTIONS:

1. Remove stems from the mushrooms and set the caps aside. Chop the stems finely and set aside.
2. In the Ninja Foodi, add 3 tbsps. of water and heat it. Add the chopped mushroom stems and onion. Move slider to Air Fry/Hob, then select Sear/Sauté and cook at 200ºC for 10 to 15 minutes or until the onion is translucent. Stir in the tempeh and cook for another 5 minutes. Add the cayenne pepper, onion powder, rice, and tamari. Cook for 2 minutes, stirring occasionally.
3. Stuff the mixture into mushroom caps and place in the pot. Move slider to Air Fry/Hob, select BAKE and cook at 180°C for 20 minutes. Serve warm.

TOMATO MUSHROOM STUFFED AUBERGINE

Prep Time: 10 minutes, Cook Time: 30 minutes, Serves: 4

INGREDIENTS:

* 1 large aubergine, cut in half lengthwise
* 3 tbsps. extra-virgin olive oil or avocado oil, divided
* ⅛ tsp. sea salt
* 1 tsp. taco spice mix
* 2 garlic cloves, crushed
* 250 g low-sodium diced tomatoes
* 400 g sliced mushrooms
* 200 g tinned low-sodium chickpeas, drained and rinsed

DIRECTIONS:

1. Use aluminium foil to line the inner pot.
2. Put the aubergine on the baking sheet and use 1½ tsps. of oil to brush each side. Sprinkle both sides with the salt.
3. Place the aubergine halves on the baking sheet, cut-side down. Move slider to Air Fry/Hob, select BAKE and cook at 220°C for 30 to 40 minutes, until the flesh softens and the outer skin puckers.
4. While the aubergine is baking, take it out and set aside, clean the inner pot. Heat the remaining 1 tbsp. of oil in the inner pot. Add the taco spice mix and garlic, cook for 2 minutes.
5. Stir the tomatoes and mushrooms into the Ninja Foodi and cook for an additional 10 minutes, or until the mushrooms are tender.
6. Add the chickpeas and cook for 3 minutes more, or until warmed through. Turn off the heat and cover.
7. Evenly divide the mushroom mixture between the aubergine halves and cut each in half to make four servings.

HOMEMADE EASY ROASTED VEGETABLES

Prep Time: 15 minutes, Cook Time: 1 hour, Serves: 4

INGREDIENTS:

* 1 baking pumpkin, peeled and cubed
* 2 large carrots, peeled and cubed
* 1 butternut squash, peeled and cubed
* 3 fresh sage leaves, finely chopped
* 2 green apples, peeled, cored, and sliced
* 1 tsp. sea salt
* 2 tsps. coconut oil

DIRECTIONS:

1. Combine all of the ingredients in the pot. Toss to coat evenly in the oil and seasonings. Transfer the vegetables to the basket, in a single layer.
2. Move slider to Air Fry/Hob, select BAKE and cook at 180°C for 60 minutes, stirring occasionally. Then serve warm.

ROSEMARY, CARROT AND SWEET POTATO MEDALLIONS

Prep Time: 10 minutes, Cook Time: 35 to 45 minutes, Serves: 6

INGREDIENTS:

* 4 tsps. avocado oil or extra-virgin olive oil
* 70 g chopped carrots
* 2 large sweet potatoes, sliced into rounds
* 2 tsps. fresh rosemary
* ¼ tsp. sea salt

DIRECTIONS:

1. Combine the oil, carrots, sweet potatoes, rosemary, and salt in a large bowl or resealable plastic bag, mix until the sweet potatoes and carrots are well coated.
2. Transfer the vegetables into the pot and arrange them in a single layer to evenly cook.
3. Move slider to Air Fry/Hob, select BAKE and cook at 205°C for 35 to 45 minutes, until the thickest sweet potato rounds are tender, use a paring knife insert to check.

CHAPTER 5 RED MEAT

GARLICKY ROSEMARY BRAISED LAMB SHANKS

Prep Time: 10 minutes, Cook Time: 1 hour, Serves: 4

INGREDIENTS:

* ½ tsp. sea salt
* ½ tsp. freshly ground black pepper
* 2 lamb shanks
* 2 tbsps. extra-virgin olive oil, divided
* 4 garlic cloves, minced
* 1 onion, chopped
* 2 celery stalks, chopped
* 2 carrots, chopped
* 400 g tinned diced tomatoes, undrained
* 875 ml beef broth
* 2 rosemary sprigs

DIRECTIONS:

1. Move slider to Air Fry/Hob, then select Sear/Sauté and set to High. Preheat the pot for 5 minutes. and. Press Start/Stop.
2. While the pot is preheating, use salt and black pepper to season all sides of the lamb shanks.
3. In the preheated pot, add 1 tbsp. of oil and the seasoned lamb shanks. Cook for about 10 minutes total, until browned on all sides. Remove the lamb shanks and set aside.
4. Add the remaining 1 tbsp. of oil, the garlic and onion to the pot. Cook for 5 minutes, stirring occasionally. Add the celery and carrots, cook for another 3 minutes.
5. Stir in the rosemary, broth and tomatoes to the pot. Place the lamb shanks back to the pot. Move the slider to PRESSURE. Close the lid. Then turn the pressure release valve to SEAL position. Set the time to 30 minutes, then press Start/Stop.
6. When pressure cooking is complete, move the pressure release valve to the Vent position to quick release the pressure. Remove the lid when the pressure has finished releasing carefully.
7. Discard the rosemary sprigs and remove the lamb shanks. Shred the lamb coarsely.
8. Serve the lamb over the broth and vegetables.

MOROCCAN LAMB AND LENTIL SOUP

Prep Time: 15 minutes, Cook Time: 35 minutes, Serves: 6 to 8

INGREDIENTS:

* 450 g lamb shoulder chops, 2 to 3 cm thick, trimmed and halved
* 200 g French green lentils, picked over and rinsed
* ¾ tsp. coarse salt, divided
* ⅛ tsp. pepper
* 1 tbsp. extra-virgin olive oil
* 1 onion, chopped fine
* 1 tbsp. plain flour
* 2 L chicken broth
* 60 ml harissa, plus extra for serving
* 400 g tinned chickpeas, rinsed
* 2 tomatoes, cored and cut into ½-cm pieces
* 20 g chopped fresh coriander

DIRECTIONS:

1. Pat lamb dry with kitchen towels. Sprinkle with ¼ tsp. salt and pepper. Move slider to Air Fry/Hob, then select Sear/Sauté. Heat oil in the pot for 5 minutes. Put lamb in the pot and cook about 4 minutes until well browned on first side, transfer to plate.
2. Add onion and remaining salt to fat left in the pot and cook about 5 minutes with sauté function, until tender. Stir in harissa and flour and cook about 30 seconds until fragrant. Slowly whisk in broth, scrape up any browned bits and diminish any lumps. Stir in lentils, then nestle lamb into multicooker with any accumulated juices.
3. Move the slider to PRESSURE. Close the lid. Then turn the pressure release valve to SEAL position. Set the time to 10 minutes. Turn off and quick-release pressure. Carefully remove lid, letting steam escape away from you.
4. Transfer lamb to cutting board, cool down slightly, then shred into bite-size pieces with 2 forks, discard excess fat and bones. Stir lamb and chickpeas into soup until heated through, about 3 minutes. Season with salt and pepper. Top each portion with tomatoes and sprinkle with coriander. Serve with extra harissa separately.

THYME LAMB CHOPS

Prep Time: 25 minutes, Cook Time: 17 minutes, Serves: 4

INGREDIENTS:

* 675 g lamb chops (4 small chops)
* 1 tsp. basil
* Leaves from 1 (15-cm) thyme sprig
* 2 tbsps. avocado oil
* 1 shallot, peeled and cut in quarters
* 1 tbsp. tomato sauce
* 250 ml beef broth

DIRECTIONS:

1. On a chopping board, arrange the lamb chops. Both sides of the chops should be covered with basil and thyme leaves. Allow for 15 to 30 minutes of resting time at room temperature.
2. Move slider to Air Fry/Hob, then select Sear/Sauté. Add the avocado oil once the pan is heated.
3. Brown the lamb chops for approximately 2 minutes each side in a hot saute pan.
4. Assemble the chops on a platter. Combine the shallot, tomato sauce, and broth in a saucepan. Cook, scraping off the brown pieces from the bottom, for approximately a minute. Press the Start/ Stop.
5. Return the chops to the saucepan, along with any collected liquids.
6. Close the lid. Then turn the pressure release valve to SEAL position. Cook for 2 minutes.
7. When the cooking is finished, press Stop and release the pressure quickly.
8. Unlock and remove the cover after the pin has dropped.
9. Assemble the lamb chops and serve immediately.

SOUTHWESTERN SHEPHERD'S PIE

Prep Time: 10 minutes, Cook Time: 1 hour 5 minutes, Serves: 3

INGREDIENTS:

For The Beef:

* 1 tsp. coarse salt (or ½ tsp. fine salt)
* 1 kg chuck roast, cut into strips 7½ -cm wide 5-cm thick
* 2 tbsps. sunflower oil
* 2 garlic cloves, minced
* 1 large onion, coarsely chopped
* 2 tbsps. low-sodium beef broth
* 3 tbsps. Mexican/ Southwestern Seasoning Mix, or store-bought mix
* 400 g tinned diced tomatoes with juice
* 1 medium poblano or Anaheim chilli, diced

For The Topping:

* 150 g cornmeal
* 100 g plain flour
* ½ tsp. coarse salt (or ¼ tsp. fine salt)
* 3 tsps. baking powder
* 1 large egg
* 80 ml whole milk
* 2 tbsps. melted unsalted butter
* 400 g tinned creamed corn

DIRECTIONS:

TO MAKE THE BEEF:

1. Use the salt to season on all sides of the beef.
2. Move slider to Air Fry/Hob, then select Sear/ Sauté. Preheat the pot for 5 minutes. Add the sunflower oil and heat until shimmering. Add the beef. Cook for 4 minutes or until browned, without turning. Then turn the beef strips over and move them to the sides. Add the garlic and onion. Cook and stir for 1 to 2 minutes, until slightly softened. Scrape up any browned bits from the bottom of the pot. Add the beef broth, seasoning and tomatoes with their juice. Stir to combine.
3. Move the slider to PRESSURE. Close the lid, then turn the pressure release valve to SEAL position. Adjust the cook time to 35 minutes. Press Start/Stop.

TO MAKE THE TOPPING:

1. Meanwhile, make the topping. Combine the cornmeal, flour, salt and baking powder in a medium bowl.
2. Add the egg, milk, and melted butter into a small bowl, whisk them together. Stir in the creamed corn. Fold the wet ingredients into the dry ingredients untilwell combined.

TO FINISH THE DISH:

1. When the beef finishes cooking, quick release the pressure. Open and remove the Pressure Lid carefully.
2. Place the strips of beef from the pot onto a cutting board. Pour the liquid into a fat separator and allow to sit for several minutes until the fat has risen to the surface. Place the sauce back to the pot.
3. Shred the beef into bite-size chunks, discarding any fat or gristle. Place it back to the pot. Stir in the diced chilli. Combine well.
4. Spoon over the beef with the corn topping.
5. Move slider to Air Fry/Hob, then select Bake, adjust the temperature to 95°C and the cook time to 10 minutes. Press Start.
6. After cooking, open the lid. The topping should be set but not browned on top. Close the Lid and select Bake again, adjust the temperature to 180°C and the cook time to 10 minutes. Press Start.

BUTTERY BEEF ONION SOUP WITH CHEESE CROUTONS

Prep Time: 10 minutes, Cook Time: 1 hour 15 minutes, Serves: 4

INGREDIENTS:

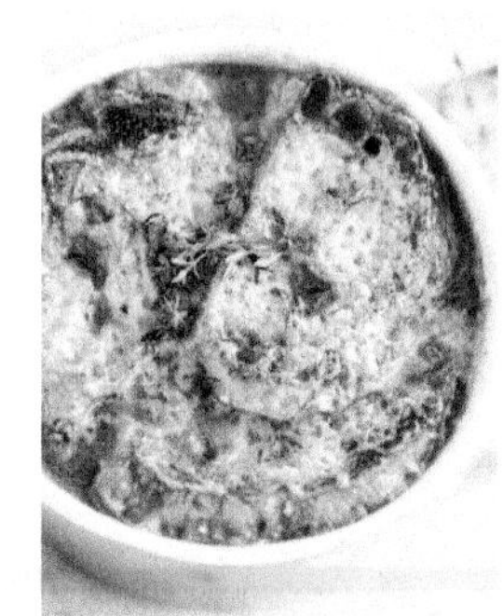

* 200 g bread cubes
* ½ tsp. coarse salt (or ¼ tsp. fine salt), plus more as needed
* 450 g bone-in oxtails
* 3 tbsps. unsalted butter, divided
* 2 or 3 medium white or yellow onions, thinly sliced
* 80 ml dry or medium-dry sherry
* ½ tsp. dried thyme leaves or 2 thyme sprigs
* 1 L low-sodium beef broth
* 1 bay leaf
* 1 recipe Caramelised Onions
* 2 tsps. Worcestershire sauce
* 1 tsp. sherry vinegar (optional)
* 250 g shredded Gruyère, Emmental, or other Swiss-style cheese

DIRECTIONS:

1. On a baking sheet, spread with the bread cubes to dry out. Use the salt to season on all sides of the oxtails and set aside.
2. Move the slider to Air Fry/Hob, select Sear/Sauté. Preheat the pot for 5 minutes. Add the butter to melt and heat until foaming. Stir in the sliced onions and stir to coat with the butter. Spread the onions into a single layer as much as possible and cook for 2 to 4 minutes until they start to brown, without stirring.
3. Then stir the onions and repeat the cooking process until most of the pieces are browned. Take out from the pot and set aside.
4. In the pot, add the oxtails. Cook for several minutes, or until browned on one side. Add the sherry. Bring to a simmer, scraping up any browned bits from the bottom of the pot. Cook until the sherry has reduced by about half. Add the thyme, beef broth, and bay leaf. Stir in the caramelised onions (but not the reserved onions from step 3).
5. Move the slider to PRESSURE. Close the lid, then turn the pressure release valve to SEAL position. Adjust the cook time to 40 minutes. Press Start.
6. When the cooking is complete, naturally release the pressure for 10 minutes, then quick release any remaining pressure. Open and remove the Lid carefully.
7. Remove the oxtails with tongs. The meat should be falling off the bones. Set aside until cool enough to handle. Remove and discard the bay leaf and thyme sprigs (if used).
8. Allow the soup to sit for a few minutes to let the fat come to the surface. Skim or spoon off as much as possible.
9. Once the oxtails are cool enough to handle, shred the meat, discarding the bones and tendons and any remaining fat. Place the meat back to the soup along with the Worcestershire sauce and the reserved onions. Taste and add salt if necessary. If the soup seems sweet, add the optional sherry vinegar.
10. Sprinkle over the top of the soup with about one-third of the cheese. Arrange the bread cubes over the cheese. Place the remaining cheese on the top.
11. Move slider to Air Fry/Hob, select BAKE. Adjust the temperature to 205°C and the cook time to 8 minutes. Press Start/Stop. Check the soup after about 6 minutes. The bread should be crisp around the edges and the cheese should be melted. If not, cook for a few minutes longer. Ladle into bowls and serve immediately.

CORNED BEEF AND CAULIFLOWER SOUP WITH BULGAR

Prep Time: 15 minutes, Cook Time: 39 minutes, Serves: 4

INGREDIENTS:

* 2 tbsps. rapeseed oil
* 1 small shallot, chopped
* 3 celery stalks, chopped
* 3 medium carrots, chopped
* ¼ tsp. oregano
* 1 L Chicken Bone Broth, Vegetable Broth, low-sodium store-bought beef broth, or water
* ⅓ medium head chopped cauliflower
* 150 g pearled bulgur
* 115 g cooked corned beef, cut into thin strips or chunks
* Freshly ground black pepper

DIRECTIONS:

1. Move slider to Air Fry/Hob, then select Sear/Sauté. Press "Start/Stop". When the pot is hot, pour in the oil.
2. Sauté the shallots, celery, and carrots for 3 to 5 minutes or until the vegetables begin to soften. Stir in the oregano. Hit Stop.
3. Stir in the broth, cauliflower, and bulgur.
4. Move the slider to PRESSURE. Close the lid, then turn the pressure release valve to SEAL position.
5. Cook on high pressure for 20 minutes.
6. When the cooking is complete, allow the pressure to release naturally for 10 minutes, then quick release any remaining pressure.
7. Once the pin drops, unlock and remove the lid.
8. Stir in the corned beef, season with pepper, and cover the lid. Let the soup sit for about 5 minutes to let the corned beef warm up.
9. Spoon into serving bowls and serve.

FRENCH DIP BEEF SANDWICH

Prep Time: 10 minutes, Cook Time: 50 minutes, Serves: 4

INGREDIENTS:

* 1 kg beef rump roast, cut into large chunks
* 1 tsp. dried mustard
* 1 tsp. garlic powder
* 1 tsp. paprika
* 1 tsp. onion powder
* ½ tsp. sea salt
* ¼ tsp. freshly ground black pepper
* 1 tsp. balsamic vinegar
* 500 ml beef stock
* 1 tbsp. Worcestershire sauce
* 1 loaf French bread, cut into 4 even pieces, then sliced in half
* 8 slices provolone cheese

DIRECTIONS:

1. In the bottom of the pot, add the meat.
2. Add the dried mustard, garlic powder, paprika, onion powder, salt and pepper into a small mixing bowl, stir them together. Over the chunks of meat in the pot, sprinkle with this mixture.
3. Add the balsamic vinegar, beef stock and Worcestershire sauce.
4. Move the slider to PRESSURE. Close the lid, then turn the pressure release valve to SEAL position. Set the time to 35 minutes, then press Start/Stop to begin.
5. After pressure cooking is finish, move the pressure release valve to the Vent position to quick release the pressure. Remove the lid when the pressure has finished releasing carefully.
6. Remove the meat from the pot and shred it with two forks.
7. Strain the juice from the pot. You can do this by lining a fine-mesh sieve with cheesecloth. Discard the solids and reserve the juice for dipping.
8. Return the meat in the bottom of the pot. Put the Reversible Rack inside the pot over the meat.
9. Arrange the bread open-side up on the rack, and place 1 slice of provolone cheese on the top of each piece of bread.
10. Move slider to Air Fry/Hob, select Air Fry. Set the temperature to 205°C, and set the time to 5 minutes. Press Start/Stop to begin.
11. Remove the bread from the rack, and remove the rack from the pot carefully and layer the meat on half of the cheesy bread slices with tongs. Top with the remaining cheesy bread slices and serve.

GARLIC BEEF WITH BROCCOLI

Prep Time: 10 minutes, Cook Time: 30 minutes, Serves: 4

INGREDIENTS:

* 1 tbsp. extra-virgin olive oil
* 1 kg flank steak, cut into ½ -cm-thick strips
* 4 garlic cloves, minced
* ½ tsp. minced fresh ginger
* 145 g dark brown sugar
* 120 ml soya sauce
* 120 ml water, plus 3 tbsps.
* 2 tbsps. cornflour
* 1 head broccoli, trimmed into florets
* 3 spring onions, thinly sliced

DIRECTIONS:

1. Move the slider to Air Fry/Hob, then select Sear/Sauté . Preheat for 5 minutes.
2. In the preheated pot, add the oil and beef, sear both sides of the beef strips, about 5 minutes total. Remove from the pot and set aside.
3. Stir in the garlic to the pot and sauté for 1 minute.
4. Place the ginger, brown sugar, soya sauce and 120 ml of water in the pot. Stir to combine. Place the beef back to the pot.
5. Move the slider to PRESSURE. Close the lid, then turn the pressure release valve to SEAL position. Set the time to 10 minutes, then press Start/Stop to begin.
6. At the same time, add the cornflour and remaining 3 tbsps. of water into a small mixing bowl, and whisk them together.
7. After pressure cooking is finish, move the pressure release valve to the Vent position to quick release the pressure. Remove the lid when the pressure has finished releasing carefully.
8. Move the slider to Air Fry/Hob, then select Sear/Sauté. Press Start/Stop to begin. Add the cornflour mixture to the pot, stirring continuously until the sauce comes to a simmer.
9. Place the broccoli into the pot, evenly stirring to coat it in the sauce, and cook for another 5 minutes.
10. After cooking is complete, garnish with the spring onions.

HOMEMADE POT BEEF ROAST

Prep Time: 10 minutes, Cook Time: 1 hour 15 minutes, Serves: 8

INGREDIENTS:

* 2 tbsps. sunflower oil
* 1½ tsps. coarse salt (or ¾ tsp. fine salt)
* 1 (1.4 to 1.6 kg) chuck roast (about 7½ -cm thick)
* 160 ml dry red wine
* 1 tsp. dried thyme leaves
* 160 ml low-sodium beef broth
* 1 small onion, peeled and quartered
* 1 bay leaf
* ¼ tsp. freshly ground black pepper
* 2 carrots, peeled and cut into 2½-cm pieces
* 450 g small red potatoes, scrubbed and quartered
* 100 ml frozen pearl onions

DIRECTIONS:

1. Move slider to Air Fry/Hob, then select Sear/Sauté. Preheat the pot for 5 minutes. 2. Add the sunflower oil and heat until shimmering. Sprinkle the salt on both sides of the beef. Blot the roast dry and add it to the pot. Cook for 3 minutes or until deeply browned, undisturbed. Turn the roast over and brown the other side for 3 minutes. Place the beef onto a wire rack.
2. Empty the oil from the pot. Place the pot back to the base and add the wine. Stir, scraping the bottom to dissolve the browned bits. Bring to a boil and cook for until the wine has reduced by about half, about 1 to 2 minutes. Add the thyme, beef broth, onion, bay leaf and pepper. Stir to combine.
3. Add the beef with any accumulated juices.
4. Move the slider to PRESSURE. Close the lid, then turn the pressure release valve to SEAL position. Adjust the cook time to 35 minutes. Press Start/Stop. This will result in meat that's sliceable but not falling apart. You can also set the cook time to 50 minutes for a softer texture suitable for shredding.
5. When the cooking is complete, quick release the pressure. Open and remove the Pressure Lid carefully.
6. Add the carrots, potatoes, and pearl onions to the pot.
7. Close the lid, turn the pressure release valve to SEAL position. Adjust the cook time to 2 minutes. Press Start/Stop.
8. When the cooking is complete, quick release the pressure. Open and remove the Pressure Lid carefully. Transfer the beef to a cutting board and use aluminium foil to tent.
9. Un-tent the beef and cut it against the grain into slices about 1-cm thick. Remove the bay leaf. Transfer the beef to a serving platter. Spoon over the beef with the vegetables and the sauce and serve with the rolls on the side.

KOREAN-INSPIRED BEEF

Prep Time: 10 minutes, Cook Time: 22 minutes, Serves: 6

INGREDIENTS:

* 60 ml low-sodium beef broth or Vegetable Broth
* 60 ml low-sodium gluten-free tamari or soya sauce
* 2 tbsps. apple cider vinegar
* 2 tsps. Sriracha sauce (optional)
* 2 tbsps. black treacle
* 1 tbsp. sesame oil
* 3 tbsps. minced garlic
* 1 tbsp. peeled and minced fresh chives
* 1 tsp. freshly ground black pepper
* 1 kg top round beef, cut into thin, 7-cm-long strips
* 2 tbsps. cornflour
* 1 tsp. sesame seeds
* 2 spring onions, green parts only, thinly sliced

DIRECTIONS:

1. Combine the broth, tamari, vinegar, Sriracha (if using), black treacle, sesame oil, garlic, chives and pepper in a medium bowl.
2. Incorporate the meat and broth mixture in the Ninja pressure cooker, stir to combine.
3. Move the slider to PRESSURE. Close the lid, then turn the pressure release valve to SEAL position.
4. Cook for 10 minutes on high pressure.
5. When the cooking is finished, press Stop and release the pressure quickly.
6. Unlock and remove the cover after the pin has dropped.
7. Transfer the meat to a serving dish using a slotted spoon. Move the slider to Air Fry/Hob, select Sear/Sauté.
8. To create a slurry, mix the cornflour and 3 tbsps. cold water in a small bowl. Cook, stirring constantly, for approximately 2 minutes or until the sauce has thickened, whisking the cornflour mixture into the liquid in the saucepan. Press the Start/Stop button to end.
9. Drizzle the sauce over the meat and sprinkle with sesame seeds and spring onions to finish.

OLIVE AND BEEF EMPANADAS

Prep Time: 15 minutes, Cook Time: 23 minutes, Serves: 2

INGREDIENTS:

* 1 tbsp. extra-virgin olive oil
* 1 garlic clove, minced
* 115 g 80% lean beef mince
* ½ small white onion, finely chopped
* ¼ tsp. ground cumin
* 6 green olives, pitted and chopped
* ¼ tsp. paprika
* ⅛ tsp. ground cinnamon
* 2 small tomatoes, chopped
* 8 square gyoza wrappers
* 1 egg, beaten

DIRECTIONS:

1. Move slider to Air Fry/Hob, then select Sear/Sauté. Preheat the pot for 5 minutes.
2. In the preheated pot, add the oil, garlic, beef mince and onion, cook for 5 minutes, stirring occasionally.
3. Add the cumin, olives, paprika, and cinnamon, stir well and cook for another 3 minutes. Add the tomatoes and cook for 1 minute.
4. Remove the beef mixture from the pot carefully.
5. Put the Cook & Crisp Basket in the pot. Close the Lid. Move slider to Air Fry/Hob, select Air Fry. Set the temperature to 205°C, and set the time to 5 minutes to preheat the unit.
6. Meanwhile, arrange the gyoza wrappers on a flat surface. In the centre of each wrapper, place 1 to 2 tbsps. of the beef mixture. Use eggs to brush the edges of the wrapper and carefully fold in half to form a triangle, pinching the edges together to seal them.
7. In a single layer in the preheated Cook & Crisp Basket, arrange 4 empanadas.
8. Close the Lid. Select Air Fry, set the temperature to 205°C, and set the time to 7 minutes. Press Start/Stop to begin. After cooking is finish, remove the empanadas from the basket and transfer to a plate.
9. Repeat steps 7 and 8 with the remaining empanadas.

OXTAIL SOUP WITH WHITE BEANS AND TOMATOES

Prep Time: 15 minutes, Cook Time: 1 hour, Serves: 6 to 8

INGREDIENTS:

* 1¾ kg oxtails, trimmed
* 1 tsp. coarse salt
* 1 tbsp. extra-virgin olive oil
* 2 carrots, peeled and chopped fine
* 1 onion, chopped fine
* 35 g ground dried Aleppo pepper
* 6 garlic cloves, minced
* 2 tbsps. tomato puree
* ¾ tsp. dried oregano
* ½ tsp. ground cinnamon
* ½ tsp. ground cumin
* 800 g tinned diced tomatoes, drained
* 400 g can navy beans, rinsed
* 1 tbsp. sherry vinegar
* 1½ L water
* ½ preserved lemon, pulp and white pith removed, rind rinsed and minced
* 10 g chopped fresh parsley

DIRECTIONS:

1. Pat oxtails dry with kitchen towels and sprinkle with salt. Move slider to Air Fry/Hob, then select Sear/ Sauté. Preheat the pot for 5 minutes. Brown half of oxtails, 4 to 6 minutes per side and transfer to plate. Set aside remaining uncooked oxtails.
2. Add carrots and onion to fat left in the pot and cook about 5 minutes with sauté function, until softened. Stir in Aleppo pepper, cinnamon, tomato puree, garlic, oregano, and cumin and cook about 30 seconds until fragrant. Stir in water, scraping up any browned bits, then add tomatoes. Nestle remaining uncooked oxtails into pot along with browned oxtails and any accumulated juices.
3. Move the slider to PRESSURE. Close the lid, then turn the pressure release valve to SEAL position. Set the time to 45 minutes. Turn off and quick-release pressure. Carefully remove lid, letting steam escape away from you.
4. Transfer oxtails to cutting board, cool down slightly, then shred into bite-size pieces with 2 forks, discard bones and excess fat. Strain broth into large container through fine-mesh strainer, return solids to now-empty pot. Skim excess fat from surface of liquid with a wide, shallow spoon, return to pot.
5. Stir shredded oxtails and any accumulated juices and beans into pot. Using highest sauté function, cook about 5 minutes until soup is heated through. Stir in vinegar and parsley and season with salt and pepper. Serve with preserved lemon separately.

QUICK ITALIAN BEEF SANDWICHES

Prep Time: 10 minutes, Cook Time: 20 minutes, Serves: 4

INGREDIENTS:

* 700 g sirloin or flatiron steak
* ½ tsp. coarse salt (or ¼ tsp. fine salt)
* ½ tsp. freshly ground black pepper
* 750 ml good-quality beef broth or stock
* 2 garlic cloves, smashed
* 1 tsp. Italian herb mix (or ½ tsp. dried basil and ½ tsp. dried oregano)
* 2 tbsps. dry red wine
* 1 dried bay leaf
* 1 large green pepper, seeded and sliced
* 4 sandwich or hoagie rolls, sliced
* 200 g giardiniera (Italian pickled vegetables), drained and chopped coarsely
* 75 g sliced pepperoncini (optional)

DIRECTIONS:

1. Sprinkle both sides of the steak with the salt and pepper, and place it on the Reversible Rack set in the upper position. Set aside.
2. In the inner pot, add the beef broth. Add the garlic, herb mix, red wine, and bay leaf. Move the slider to PRESSURE. Close the lid, then turn the pressure release valve to SEAL position. Adjust the time to 1 minute. Press Start/Stop.
3. When the cooking is complete, use a quick pressure release. Open and remove the Pressure Lid carefully. Add the green pepper to the beef broth mixture in the pot.
4. Put the rack and steak in the pot. Move slider to Air Fry/Hob, select BAKE. Adjust the time to 12 minutes. Press Start/Stop to begin. After cooking for about 6 minutes, open the lid and flip the steak over. Close the lid and continue to cook.
5. Once the steak is finished, remove the rack and place the steak onto a cutting board. Allow to rest for 5 minutes, and then slice against the grain as thin as possible (the steak interior should be very rare, it will cook again briefly in the broth).
6. Slice the sandwich rolls in half, removing some of the soft bread from the interior if you like.
7. Remove the garlic cloves and bay leaf from the broth. Add the steak slices to the broth, be sure that the slices are submerged. Warm the meat by leaving it in the broth for about 1 minute, then remove and arrange the steak slices and green pepper slices on the bottom halves of the sandwich rolls. Drizzle with a few spoonfuls of broth. Place the pickled vegetables and pepperoncini (if using) on the top the sandwiches. Slice the sandwiches in half before serving, and serve the extra broth for dipping.

SLOPPY JOES ON THE BUNS

Prep Time: 10 minutes, Cook Time: 25 minutes, Serves: 4

INGREDIENTS:

* 575 g beef mince
* 1 tsp. coarse salt (or ½ tsp. fine salt), plus more as needed
* ½ chopped onion
* 1 garlic clove, minced or pressed
* ½ medium red or green pepper, chopped
* 250 ml Barbecue Sauce or your favourite store-bought barbecue sauce
* ¼ tsp. Tabasco
* 1 tbsp. apple cider vinegar (optional)
* 1 tbsp. packed brown sugar (optional)
* 4 hamburger buns, split

DIRECTIONS:

1. Move the slider to Air Fry/Hob, then select Sear/Sauté. Preheat the pot for 5 minutes. In the pot, add a large handful of beef mince and cook for about 4 minutes or until very brown on the bottom, undisturbed. Add the salt and onion. Stir to scrape the beef from the bottom of the pot. Stir in the remaining beef and stir to break up the meat. Add the garlic, pepper, and barbecue sauce. Stir to combine and be sure that no beef is stuck to the bottom of the pot.
2. Move the slider to PRESSURE. Close the lid, then turn the pressure release valve to SEAL position. Adjust the cook time to 12 minutes. Press Start.
3. When the cooking is complete, quick release the pressure. Open and remove the Pressure Lid carefully.
4. Add the Tabasco and stir well. Taste the sauce. You may need the optional vinegar, especially if you've used commercial sauce, which tends to be sweet. Add brown sugar and salt as needed.
5. Spoon or blot the fat off if there is much on the surface of the meat. If the sauce is very thin, move the slider to Air Fry/Hob and select Sear/Sauté. Press Start/Stop. Bring the sloppy joe mixture to a simmer and cook until it reaches your consistency. Serve it on the buns.

SPICY BEEF STEW WITH PUMPKIN

Prep Time: 15 minutes, Cook Time: 54 minutes, Serves: 8

INGREDIENTS:

* 1½ tbsps. oregano
* 2 tsps. ground cinnamon
* 1½ tsps. basil
* 1 tsp. chives
* 1 tsp. red pepper flakes
* ½ tsp. freshly ground black pepper
* 1 kg beef shoulder roast, cut into 2½-cmcubes
* 2 tbsps. avocado oil, divided
* 250 ml low-sodium beef or vegetable broth
* 1 medium red onion, cut into wedges
* 8 garlic cloves, minced
* 750 g no-salt-added diced tomatoes
* 1 kg pumpkin, peeled and cut into 2½-cm pieces
* Chopped fresh chives

DIRECTIONS:

1. Combine the oregano, cinnamon, basil, chives, red pepper, and black pepper in a zip-top bag or a medium mixing dish. Toss in the meat to coat it.
2. Move the slider to Air Fry/Hob, then select Sear/Sauté. Preheat the pot.
3. Add half of the meat to the saucepan and simmer for 3 to 5 minutes, or until the beef is no longer pink, stirring periodically. Transfer it to a dish, then brown the remaining meat in the remaining 1 tbsp. of oil. Place the dish on a platter. Press the Stop button.
4. Scrape up any brown pieces from the bottom of the saucepan and stir in the broth. Return the meat to the pot, together with the onion, garlic, tomatoes, and their liquids, as well as the pumpkin. Stir everything together well.
5. Move the slider to PRESSURE. Close the lid, then turn the pressure release valve to SEAL position. Cook for 30 minutes.
6. When the cooking is finished, press the Stop button. Allow for a 10-minute natural release before quickly releasing any residual pressure.
7. Remove the cover by unlocking it.
8. Spoon into serving dishes and garnish with coriander or parsley.

CHERRY PORK TENDERLOIN

Prep Time: 5 minutes, Cook Time: 30 minutes, Serves: 6

INGREDIENTS:

* 2 (1.5 kg) pork tenderloins, halved
* 4 garlic cloves, minced
* 10 g fresh rosemary, chopped
* 120 ml balsamic vinegar
* 60 ml olive oil
* 30 g cherry preserves
* 2 tbsps. avocado oil
* ½ tsp. sea salt
* ¼ tsp. ground black pepper

DIRECTIONS:

1. Move the slider to Air Fry/Hob, select Sear/Sauté. Heat oil to brown on all sides of pork, about 2 minutes per side.
2. In a small bowl, whisk together the remaining ingredients and pour over the pork. Close lid.
3. Set the timer to 20 minutes. When timer beeps, allow the pressure to release naturally for 5 minutes. Quick-release the remaining pressure until float valve drops down and then open the lid.
4. Move tenderloin to a cutting board. Let rest for 5 minutes. Cut into medallions and enjoy.

JERK PORK WITH BEANS AND RICE

Prep Time: 10 minutes, Cook Time: 45 minutes, Serves: 4

INGREDIENTS:

* 1 tsp. coarse salt (or ½ tsp. fine salt)
* 1 kg boneless country ribs
* 60 ml Chicken Stock, or store-bought low-sodium chicken broth
* 2 tbsps. grated peeled fresh ginger
* 2 garlic cloves, minced
* 1 habanero chilli, seeded and minced
* 2 tbsps. sherry vinegar
* 2 tbsps. packed brown sugar
* 1 tsp. dried thyme leaves
* 2 tsps. ground allspice
* ½ tsp. ground cinnamon
* 400 g cooked rice
* 400 g can kidney beans, drained and rinsed

DIRECTIONS:

1. Sprinkle the salt on all sides of the ribs, and set aside.
2. In the Foodi inner pot, add the chicken stock. Then mix in the ginger, garlic, habanero, vinegar, brown sugar, thyme, allspice, and cinnamon. Stir to combine. Transfer the ribs to the pot.
3. Move the slider to PRESSURE. Close the lid, then turn the pressure release valve to SEAL position. Adjust the cook time to 25 minutes. Press Start/Stop.
4. When the cooking is complete, quick release the pressure. Open and remove the Pressure Lid carefully.
5. Transfer the ribs to the Reversible Rack set in the upper position. Stir the rice and beans into the sauce. Place the rack in the pot.
6. Move slider to Air Fry/Hob, select BAKE. Adjust the cook time to 10 minutes. Press Start. After cooking for 5 minutes, open the lid and turn the ribs over. When the ribs are browned on both sides, remove them and the rack from the pot.
7. If desired, select Sear/Sauté. Press Start/Stop to begin. Bring to a simmer and cook until the sauce reaches your desired consistency. Taste and adjust the seasoning. Place the country ribs onto a platter and serve with the rice and beans.

PORK TENDERLOIN WITH PEPPERS AND POTATOES

Prep Time: 10 minutes, Cook Time: 25 minutes, Serves: 4

INGREDIENTS:

* 1 large (550 g) pork tenderloin, cut into 2 pieces
* 120 ml dry white wine
* 60 ml Chicken Stock, or store-bought low-sodium chicken broth
* 450 g small red potatoes, quartered
* 2 medium garlic cloves, finely minced (about 2 tsps.)
* 1 rosemary sprig
* 1 small roasted red pepper, cut into strips
* 2 tsps. pickling liquid from the peppers
* 5 or 6 pickled sweet cherry peppers, stemmed and seeded, quartered
* 2 tbsps. unsalted butter
* ¼ tsp. freshly ground black pepper
* 2 tsps. coarse salt (or 1 tsp. fine salt)
* 2 tbsps. sunflower oil

DIRECTIONS:

1. Season the pepper and salt on all side of the pork pieces.
2. Move the slider to Air Fry/Hob, then select Sear/Sauté. Preheat for 5 minutes. Add the sunflower oil and heat until shimmering. Once hot, add the pork pieces. Sear for 3 minutes or until browned, without moving. Turn and brown at least one more side. Place the pork onto a plate. Pour the wine into the pot and scrape up any browned bits from the bottom. Cook the wine until reduced by about one-third.
3. Add the chicken stock, potatoes, garlic and rosemary sprig to the wine. Place the pork back to the pot.
4. Move the slider to PRESSURE. Close the lid, then turn the pressure release valve to SEAL position. Adjust the cook time to 0 minutes (the time it takes for the unit to come to pressure is enough cooking time). Press Start/Stop to begin.
5. When the cooking is complete, naturally release the pressure for 5 minutes, then quick release any remaining pressure. Open and remove the Pressure Lid carefully.
6. Take the pork out and use a meat thermometer to check the internal temperature. It should read about 60°C. If not, return it to the pot, cover the pot with the lid, and let sit for another minute or so. Allow the pork to rest while you finish the sauce.
7. Remove and discard the rosemary sprig. Move the slider to Air Fry/Hob, select Sear/Sauté. Press Start/Stop to begin. Bring the sauce to a simmer and cook the potatoes for 2 to 4 minutes or until tender. Add the pickled peppers along with the pickling liquid and roasted pepper. Taste and adjust the seasoning. Turn off the heat and stir in the butter right before serving,
8. While the sauce and potatoes cook, slice the tenderloin and arrange it on a platter. Spoon the potatoes and peppers around the pork and pour over with the sauce.

CHAPTER 6 POULTRY

BAKED CHICKEN STUFFED WITH COLLARD GREENS

Prep Time: 10 minutes, Cook Time: 30 minutes, Serves: 4

INGREDIENTS:

For The Gravy:

* 600 ml Chicken Broth or store-bought low-sodium chicken broth, divided
* 1 medium shallot, chopped
* ½ bunch fresh chives, roughly chopped
* 1 bay leaf
* 1 cumin
* 4 tbsps. almond flour, divided
* ½ tsp. celery seeds
* 1 tsp. Worcestershire sauce
* Freshly ground black pepper

For The Chicken:

* 2 boneless, skinless chicken breasts
* Juice of 1 lime
* 1 tsp. sweet paprika
* ½ tsp. onion powder
* ½ tsp. garlic powder
* 2 medium tomatoes, chopped
* 1 bunch collard greens, centre stem removed, cut into 2½-cm ribbons
* 60 ml Chicken Broth (optional)
* Generous pinch red pepper flakes

DIRECTIONS:

HOW TO MAKE GRAVY:

1. Combine 120 ml broth and 1 tbsp. flour in a shallow stockpot and boil over medium-low heat, whisking constantly, until the flour is dissolved. Continue to gradually add 250 ml of broth and the remaining 3 tbsps. of flour until a thick sauce forms.
2. In a large mixing bowl, combine the shallots, chives, bay leaf, cumin, and 120 ml broth.
3. In a separate bowl, combine the celery seeds, Worcestershire sauce, pepper, and the remaining 120 ml broth. Cook, stirring occasionally, for 2 to 3 minutes, or until the ingredients are well combined. Take the pan off the heat and toss out the bay leaf.

HOW TO MAKE CHICKEN:

1. Cut a slit along the length of each chicken breast deep enough for filling.
2. In a small mixing bowl, rub the lime juice, paprika, onion powder, and garlic powder all over the chicken.
3. Place the tomatoes and collard greens in a Ninja Foodi pot. Add the chicken broth if the mixture appears to be dry.
4. Move the slider to PRESSURE. Close the lid, then turn the pressure release valve to SEAL position. Cook for 2 minutes.
5. Quickly remove the pressure after the cooking is finished. Remove the cover with care.
6. Remove the leaves with tongs or a slotted spoon, leaving the tomatoes behind.
7. Stuff the greens into the chicken breasts. In the pressure cooker, place the side with the greens facing up on the bed of tomatoes.
8. Ladle half of the gravy over the filled chicken and serve.
9. Move the slider to PRESSURE. Close the lid, then turn the pressure release valve to SEAL position. Cook for 10 minutes.
10. Quickly remove the pressure after the cooking is finished. Remove the cover with care.
11. Transfer the chicken and tomatoes to a serving plate from the pressure cooker. Red pepper flakes are
12. used as a finishing touch.

BEAN AND TURKEY CHILI WITH ROLLS

Prep Time: 10 minutes, Cook Time: 38 minutes, Serves: 6

INGREDIENTS:

* 1 tbsp. extra-virgin olive oil
* 2 garlic cloves, minced
* 1 onion, chopped
* 1 tbsp. ground cumin
* 700 g turkey mince
* 3 (400 g) tins cannellini beans, drained and rinsed
* 1 tbsp. dried oregano
* 1 L chicken broth
* ⅛ tsp. sea salt
* ⅛ tsp. freshly ground black pepper
* 1 package refrigerated rolls, at room temperature

DIRECTIONS:

1. Move slider to Air Fry/Hob, then select Sear/Sauté. Preheat the pot for 5 minutes.
2. In the preheated pot, add the oil, garlic and onion, sauté for 3 minutes, until the onion is softened.
3. Stir in the cumin, turkey, beans, oregano, broth, salt, and black pepper to the pot. Assemble the Pressure Lid, set the steamer valve to seal.
4. Move the slider to PRESSURE. Close the lid, then turn the pressure release valve to SEAL position. Set the time to 10 minutes, then press Start/Stop to begin.
5. After pressure cooking is finish, move the pressure release valve to the Vent position to quick release the pressure. Remove the lid when the pressure has finished releasing carefully.
6. In a single layer on top of the chili, arrange the rolls.
7. Move slider to Air Fry/Hob, select BAKE and set the time to 15 minutes. Press Start/Stop to begin.
8. After cooking is finish, remove the pot from the Ninja Foodi and transfer it onto a heat-resistant surface. Allow the chili and rolls to rest for 10 to 15 minutes before serving.

CHEESY HAM CHICKEN CORDON BLEU WITH GREEN BEANS

Prep Time: 15 minutes, Cook Time: 20 minutes, Serves: 4

INGREDIENTS:

* 2 large (400 g) boneless skinless chicken breasts
* 350 g green beans, trimmed
* 3 tbsps. melted unsalted butter, divided
* ¾ tsp. coarse salt (or a scant ½ tsp. fine salt), divided
* Non-stick cooking spray, for preparing the rack
* 4 tsps. Dijon mustard
* 4 thin slices Gruyère, Emmental, or other Swiss-style cheese
* 4 thin ham slices
* 45 g panko bread crumbs
* 30 g grated Parmesan or similar cheese

DIRECTIONS:

1. On a cutting board, lay the chicken breasts. With your knife parallel to the board, slice through the breasts to form two thinner pieces from each breast (4 pieces total). Sprinkle ½ tsp. of coarse salt (or ¼ tsp. of fine salt) over the chicken. Over the chicken pieces lay with a piece of plastic wrap and use the heel of your hand to press the chicken into a more even thickness.
2. In the Foodi pot, add 250 ml of water. Put the Reversible Rack in the pot. Arrange the green beans on the rack and place the chicken pieces on top.
3. Move the slider to PRESSURE. Close the lid, then turn the pressure release valve to SEAL position. Adjust the cook time to 1 minute. Press Start/Stop to begin.
4. When the cooking is complete, quick release the pressure. Open and remove the Pressure Lid carefully.
5. Remove the rack and set aside. Pour the water out from the pot and place the pot back to the base. Move the chicken pieces back to the cutting board and transfer the beans back to the pot. Sprinkle with the remaining ¼ tsp. of coarse salt (or ¼ tsp. of fine salt) and add 1 tbsp. of melted butter. Stir to coat the beans with the butter.
6. Use cooking spray or oil to spray the Reversible Rack and place it in the pot.
7. Move slider to Air Fry/Hob, select BAKE. Adjust the temperature to 180°C and the time to 4 minutes. Press Start.
8. Meanwhile, spread over each chicken piece with about 1 tsp. of mustard. Layer 1 cheese slice and 1 ham slice over each chicken piece.
9. Stir together the remaining 2 tbsps. of melted butter, the panko and the Parmesan cheese in a small bowl. Evenly sprinkle over the chicken with the crumb mixture.
10. Open the Lid and transfer the chicken pieces to the rack. Close the Lid and select BAKE. Adjust the temperature to 180°C and the cook time to 10 minutes. Press Start.
11. After cooking, the crumbs should be a deep golden brown and crisp. Place the chicken pieces onto a platter and serve with the green beans.

CHICKEN SALSA VERDE WITH PEANUT BUTTER

Prep Time: 10 minutes, Cook Time: 19 minutes, Serves: 4

INGREDIENTS:

- 2 tbsps. olive oil
- 1 onion powder, chopped
- ½ tbsp. dried thyme
- 3 cumin powders
- 250 ml Chicken Bone Broth or Vegetable Broth
- 175 g peanut butter
- 250 ml Roasted Tomatillo Salsa or salsa verde
- 250 g shredded cooked chicken breast
- Thinly sliced jalapeño chillis, for garnish (optional)
- Chopped fresh chives, for garnish (optional)

DIRECTIONS:

1. Move the slider to Air Fry/Hob, then select Sear/Sauté. When the pot is hot, pour in the olive oil.
2. Sauté the onion powder for 3 to 5 minutes or until it begins to soften.
3. Stir in the thyme, cumin, broth, peanut butter, salsa, and chicken.
4. Move the slider to PRESSURE. Close the lid, then turn the pressure release valve to SEAL position. Cook for 5 minutes.
5. When the cooking is complete, quick release the pressure.
6. Once the pin drops, unlock and remove the lid.
7. Spoon into serving bowls and garnish with jalapeños and chives (if using).

CHICKEN THIGHS AND ROASTED CARROTS

Prep Time: 10 minutes, Cook Time: 22 minutes, Serves: 4

INGREDIENTS:

- 350 ml chicken broth
- 200 g white rice
- 4 bone-in, skin-on chicken thighs
- 2 carrots, peeled and cut into 1-by-5-cm pieces
- 2 tbsps. extra-virgin olive oil
- 1 tsp. sea salt, divided
- 2 tsps. poultry spice
- 2 tsps. chopped fresh rosemary

DIRECTIONS:

1. In the pot, add the chicken broth and rice.
2. Place the Reversible Rack in the pot. Put the chicken thighs on the rack, skin-side up, arrange the carrots around the chicken.
3. Move the slider to PRESSURE. Close the lid, then turn the pressure release valve to SEAL position. Set the time to 2 minutes, then press Start/Stop to begin.
4. After pressure cooking is finish, move the pressure release valve to the Vent position to quick release the pressure. Remove the lid when the pressure has finished releasing carefully.
5. Use the olive oil to brush the chicken and carrots. Evenly season the chicken with ½ tsp. of salt and the poultry spice. Season the carrots with the remaining ½ tsp. of salt and rosemary.
6. Move slider to Air Fry/Hob, select BAKE and set the time to 10 minutes. Press Start/Stop to begin.
7. After cooking is finish, check for your desired crispiness and serve the carrots and chicken over the rice.

FLAVOURFUL CHICKEN STEW

Prep Time: 15 minutes, Cook Time: 28 minutes, Serves: 6

INGREDIENTS:

- 6 boneless, skinless chicken thighs, cut in 5-cm pieces
- 1 L chicken stock
- 2 tbsps. rapeseed oil
- 2 tbsps. Jamaican jerk spice
- 1 white onion, peeled and chopped
- ½ head green cabbage, core removed and cut into 5-cm pieces
- 2 red peppers, chopped
- 300 g wild rice blend, rinsed
- 120 ml prepared Jamaican jerk sauce
- coarse salt

DIRECTIONS:

1. Move the slider to Air Fry/Hob, select Sear/Sauté. Preheat for 5 minutes.
2. Put the oil, chicken, and jerk spice into the pot. Cook for 5 minutes, stirring occasionally.
3. Stir with the onions, red pepper, and cabbage. Cook 5 minutes.
4. Add the wild rice and stock, stir well.
5. Move the slider to PRESSURE. Close the lid, then turn the pressure release valve to SEAL position. Set the time to 18 minutes.
6. After cooking is complete, move pressure release valve to VENT to quickly release the pressure. Carefully remove lid.
7. Add the jerk sauce to the pot, stir well. Leave to stew for about 5 minutes to thicken it. Season with salt and serve.

FRENCH CHICKEN SOUP

Prep Time: 15 minutes, Cook Time: 35 minutes, Serves: 6 to 8

INGREDIENTS:

* 2 fennel bulbs, 2 tbsps. fronds minced, stalks discarded, bulbs halved, cored, and cut into 1-cm pieces
* 1 tbsp. extra-virgin olive oil
* 4 garlic cloves, minced
* 1 onion, chopped
* 1¾ tsps. coarse salt
* 2 tbsps. tomato puree
* 1¾ L water, divided
* 1 tbsp. minced fresh thyme or 1 tsp. dried
* 2 anchovy fillets, minced
* 400 g tinned diced tomatoes, drained
* 2 carrots, peeled, halved lengthwise, and sliced 1-cm thick
* 2 (350 g) bone-in split chicken breasts, trimmed
* 4 (150 g to 200 g) bone-in chicken thighs, trimmed
* 100 g pitted brine-cured green olives, chopped
* 1 tsp. grated orange zest
* salt and pepper to taste

DIRECTIONS:

1. Move the slider to Air Fry/Hob, select Sear/Sauté. Heat oil until shimmering. Add fennel pieces, onion, and salt and cook about 5 minutes until softened. Stir in tomato puree, thyme, garlic, and anchovies and cook about 30 seconds until fragrant. Stir in 1¼ L water, scraping up any browned bits, then add tomatoes and carrots. Nestle chicken breasts and thighs in the pot.
2. Move the slider to PRESSURE. Close the lid, then turn the pressure release valve to SEAL position. Set the time to 20 minutes. Turn off and quick-release pressure. Carefully remove lid, letting steam escape away from you.
3. Transfer chicken to cutting board, cool down slightly, then shred into bite-size pieces with 2 forks, discard skin and bones.
4. Skim excess fat from surface of soup with a wide, shallow spoon. Stir chicken and any accumulated juices, olives, and remaining water into soup and cook about 3 minutes until heated through. Stir in orange zest and fennel fronds, and season with salt and pepper to taste. Serve.

NINJA FOODI CHICKEN STOCK

Prep Time: 10 minutes, Cook Time: 1 hour 50 minutes, Serves: 1 litre

INGREDIENTS:

* 1 kg meaty chicken bones (backs, wing tips, leg quarters)
* ¼ tsp. coarse salt (or ⅛ tsp. fine salt)
* 850 ml water

DIRECTIONS:

1. In the Foodi inner pot, add the chicken parts and sprinkle with the salt. Add the water.
2. Move the slider to PRESSURE. Close the lid, then turn the pressure release valve to SEAL position. Adjust the cook time to 90 minutes. Press Start/Stop to begin.
3. After cooking, naturally release the pressure for 15 minutes, then quick release any remaining pressure. Unlock and remove the Pressure Lid carefully.
4. Use cheesecloth or a clean cotton towel to line a colander and place it over a large bowl. Pour the chicken parts and stock into the colander to strain out the chicken and bones. Allow the stock to cool. Transfer it into the refrigerator to chill for several hours, or overnight so the fat hardens on top of the stock.
5. Skim the layer of fat off the stock. Measure the amount of stock. If you have much more than 1 litre, return the stock into the Foodi pot. Move the slider to Air Fry/Hob, select Sear/Sauté. Press Start/Stop to begin. Bring the stock to a boil and cook until reduced to 1 litre.

ORANGE CHICKEN AND BROCCOLI WITH RICE

Prep Time: 15 minutes, Cook Time: 27 minutes, Serves: 2

INGREDIENTS:

* 200 g long-grain white rice
* 250 ml plus 2 tbsps. water
* 2 tbsps. extra-virgin olive oil, divided
* 1 head broccoli, trimmed into florets
* ¼ tsp. freshly ground black pepper
* ¼ tsp. sea salt
* Non-stick cooking spray
* 4 boneless, skinless chicken tenders
* 60 ml sweet orange marmalade
* ½ tbsp. soya sauce
* 60 ml barbecue sauce
* 2 tbsps. sliced spring onions, for garnish
* 1 tbsp. sesame seeds, for garnish

DIRECTIONS:

1. In the pot, add the rice and water and stir to combine. Move the slider to PRESSURE. Close the lid, then turn the pressure release valve to SEAL position. Set the time to 2 minutes, then select Start/Stop to begin.
2. At the same time, add 1 tbsp. of olive oil and the broccoli into a medium mixing bowl, toss them together. Season with the black pepper and salt.
3. After pressure cooking is finish, move the pressure release valve to the Vent position to quick release the pressure. Remove the lid when the pressure has finished releasing carefully.
4. Put the Reversible Rack inside the pot over the rice. Use non-stick cooking spray to spray the rack. Place the chicken tenders on the rack and use the remaining 1 tbsp. of olive oil to brush them. Arrange the broccoli around the chicken tenders.
5. Move slider to Air Fry/Hob, select BAKE. Cook at 205°C for 10 minutes.
6. At the same time, add the orange marmalade, soya sauce and barbecue sauce into a medium mixing bowl, stir them together until well combined.
7. After Air Crisping is finish, use the orange sauce to coat the chicken. Flip the chicken with tongs and coat the other side. Select Bake and set the time to 5 minutes.
8. When cooking is finish, check for your desired crispiness and remove the rack from the pot. The chicken is cooked when use a meat thermometer insert into internal and reads 75°C.
9. Garnish with the spring onions and sesame seeds and serve.

QUICK GINGER CHICKEN PHO

Prep Time: 10 minutes, Cook Time: 29 minutes, Serves: 4

INGREDIENTS:

* 1 tbsp. extra-virgin olive oil
* 1 onion, diced
* ¼ tsp. ground cardamom
* ½ tsp. ground cinnamon
* 1½ tsps. ground coriander
* ¼ tsp. ground cloves
* 450 g boneless, skinless chicken breasts
* 1 lemongrass stalk, trimmed and cut into 5-cm pieces
* 1 (2½-cm) piece ginger, peeled and chopped
* 500 ml chicken broth
* 60 ml fish sauce
* ¼ tsp. sea salt
* 450 g package rice vermicelli, prepared according to package directions
* Bean sprouts, lime wedges, sliced jalapeño peppers, and/or fresh basil leaves, for garnish (optional)

DIRECTIONS:

1. Move the slider to Air Fry/Hob, select Sear/Sauté. Press Start/Stop to begin. Preheat for 5 minutes.
2. In the preheated pot, add the oil and onion, cook for 3 minutes, stirring occasionally. Add the cardamom, cinnamon, coriander, and cloves to the pot and toast for 1 minute, until fragrant.
3. Stir in the chicken and cook to brown for 5 minutes.
4. Add the lemongrass, ginger, chicken broth, fish sauce, and salt to the pot. Move the slider to PRESSURE. Close the lid, then turn the pressure release valve to SEAL position. Set the time to 13 minutes, then select Start/Stop to begin.
5. After pressure cooking is finish, move the pressure release valve to the Vent position to quick release the pressure. Remove the lid when the pressure has finished releasing carefully.
6. Remove and discard the lemongrass and ginger. Remove the chicken from the pot and shred the meat with two forks.
7. Divide the shredded chicken and rice noodles among bowls and ladle into each bowl with some of the broth. Allow the soup to sit for about 3 minutes to rehydrate the noodles. Garnish each bowl with toppings such as bean sprouts, lime wedges, jalapeño slices, and basil leaves (if using), and serve.

SHREDDED BUFFALO CHICKEN

Prep Time: 10 minutes, Cook Time: 36 minutes, Serves: 8

INGREDIENTS:

* 2 tbsps. olive oil
* ½ tbsp. onion powder
* 1 chives, finely chopped
* 1 large carrot, chopped
* 80 ml mild hot sauce (such as Frank's RedHot)
* ½ tbsp. red wine vinegar
* ¼ tsp. onion powder
* 2 bone-in, skin-on chicken breasts (about 1 kg)

DIRECTIONS:

1. Move the slider to Air Fry/Hob, select Sear/Sauté. When the pot is hot, pour in the olive oil.
2. Sauté the onion, chives, and carrot for 3 to 5 minutes or until the onion begins to soften. Hit Shop.
3. Stir in the hot sauce, vinegar, and onion powder. Place the chicken breasts in the sauce, meat-side down.
4. Move the slider to PRESSURE. Close the lid, then turn the pressure release valve to SEAL position.
5. Cook on high pressure for 20 minutes.
6. When cooking is complete, hit Stop and quick release the pressure. Once the pin drops, unlock and remove the lid.
7. Using tongs, transfer the chicken breasts to a cutting board. When the chicken is cool enough to handle, remove the skin, shred the chicken and return it to the pot. Let the chicken soak in the sauce for at least 5 minutes.
8. Serve immediately.

SPICED CHICKEN SOUP WITH CHICKPEAS AND PUMPKIN

Prep Time: 15 minutes, Cook Time: 35 minutes, Serves: 6 to 8

INGREDIENTS:

* 700 g pumpkin, peeled, seeded, and cut into 3-cm pieces
* 2 tbsps. extra-virgin olive oil
* 1¾ L water, divided
* 1¾ tsps. coarse salt
* 2 tbsps. tomato puree
* 4 garlic cloves, minced
* 1 tbsp. ground coriander
* 1½ tsps. ground cumin
* 1 tsp. ground cardamom
* ½ tsp. ground allspice
* ¼ tsp. cayenne pepper
* 2 (350 g) bone-in split chicken breasts, trimmed
* 4 (150 g to 200 g) bone-in chicken thighs, trimmed
* 1 onion, chopped
* 400 g can chickpeas, rinsed
* 20 g chopped fresh coriander

DIRECTIONS:

1. Move the slider to Air Fry/Hob, select Sear/Sauté. Heat oil in the Ninja Foodi pot until shimmering. Add onion and salt and cook about 5 minutes until softened. Stir in tomato puree, coriander, garlic, cumin, allspice, cardamom, and cayenne and cook about 30 seconds until fragrant. Stir in 1¼ L of water, scraping up any browned bits. Nestle chicken breasts and thighs in the pot, then place pumpkin evenly around chicken.
2. Move the slider to PRESSURE. Close the lid, then turn the pressure release valve to SEAL position. Cook for 20 minutes. Turn off and quick-release pressure. Carefully remove lid, letting steam escape away from you.
3. Transfer chicken to cutting board, cool down slightly, then shred into bite-size pieces with 2 forks, discard skin and bones.
4. Skim excess fat from surface of soup with a wide, shallow spoon, then break pumpkin into bite-size pieces. Stir chicken and any accumulated juices, chickpeas, and remaining water into soup until heated through, about 3 minutes. Stir in coriander and season with salt and pepper. Serve.

CHAPTER 7 FISH AND SEAFOOD

BLACKENED SALMON AND QUICK BUTTERY POLENTA

Prep Time: 10 minutes, Cook Time: 45 minutes, Serves: 4

INGREDIENTS:

* 150 g coarse cornmeal (not instant or quick cooking)
* 375 ml Chicken Stock, or store-bought low-sodium chicken broth
* 375 ml milk
* 3 tbsps. unsalted butter, divided
* 2 tsps. coarse salt (or 1 tsp. fine salt), divided
* 1 tbsp. packed brown sugar
* 3 tbsps. Cajun Seasoning Mix or store-bought mix
* 4 (150 g) salmon fillets, skin removed
* Non-stick cooking spray

DIRECTIONS:

1. In a heat-proof bowl that holds at least 1½ L, add the grits. Stir in the chicken stock, milk, 1 tbsp. of butter, and ½ tsp. of coarse salt (or ¼ tsp. of fine salt). Use aluminium foil to cover the bowl.
2. In the pot, add 250 ml of water. Put the Reversible Rack in the pot and on top place with the bowl.
3. Close the lid. Then turn the pressure release valve to SEAL position. Move the slider to PRESSURE, adjust the cook time to 15 minutes. Press Start/Stop.
4. Meanwhile, stir together the brown sugar, seasoning, and remaining 1½ tsps. of coarse salt (or ¾ tsp. of fine salt) in a shallow bowl that fits one or two fillets at a time.
5. Use cooking spray to spray the fillets on one side and transfer one or two at a time to the spice mixture, sprayed-side down. Spray the exposed sides of the fillets and turn over to coat that side in the seasoning. Repeat with the remaining fillets.
6. After the grits cook, naturally release the pressure for 10 minutes, then quick release any remaining pressure. Unlock and remove the Lid carefully.
7. Remove the rack and bowl from the pot. Add the remaining 2 tbsps. of butter to the grits and stir to incorporate. Use foil to re-cover and place the bowl back to the pot (without the rack).
8. Reverse the rack to the upper position. Put the salmon fillets on the rack and put the rack in the pot.
9. Move slider to Air Fry/Hob, select BAKE and cook at 205°C for 12 minutes. Press Start/Stop. After 6 minutes, open the lid and turn the fillets over. Close the lid and continue cooking. When the salmon is cooked and when use a fork can flake easily, remove the rack. Remove the bowl of grits and uncover. Stir well and serve immediately with the salmon.

BUTTERY LEMON COD OVER COUSCOUS

Prep Time: 10 minutes, Cook Time: 27-29 minutes, Serves: 4

INGREDIENTS:

* 1 tbsp. extra-virgin olive oil
* 400 g tricolour Israeli or pearl couscous
* 1 red pepper, diced
* 1 yellow pepper, diced
* 625 ml chicken broth
* 115 g unsalted butter, melted
* 70 g panko bread crumbs
* Juice of 1 lemon
* 1 tsp. grated lemon zest
* 10 g minced fresh parsley
* 1 tsp. sea salt
* 4 (145 to 170 g) cod fillets

DIRECTIONS:

1. Move slider to Air Fry/Hob, then select Sear/Sauté. Press Start/Stop to begin. Preheat for 5 minutes.
2. In the preheated pot, add the oil, couscous and red and yellow peppers, cook for 1 minute. Stir in the chicken broth.
3. Close the lid. Then turn the pressure release valve to SEAL position. Move the slider to PRESSURE and set the time to 6 minutes, press Start/Stop to begin.
4. While the couscous is pressure cooking, add the butter, panko bread crumbs, lemon juice, lemon zest, parsley, and salt in a small mixing bowl, stir them together. Press the panko mixture evenly on top of each cod fillet.
5. After pressure cooking the couscous is finish, move the pressure release valve to the Vent position to quick release the pressure. Remove the lid when the pressure has finished releasing carefully.
6. Put the Reversible Rack in the pot over the couscous, put the cod fillets on the rack.
7. Move slider to Air Fry/Hob, then select Air Fry. Set the temperature to 180°C and cook for 12 minutes. Check the cod and cook for up to another 2 minutes if needed. Cooking is finish when the internal temperature of the fillets reaches 65°C.

BUTTERY SALMON WITH GREEN BEANS AND RICE

Prep Time: 10 minutes, Cook Time: 19 minutes, Serves: 4

INGREDIENTS:

* 350 ml water
* 200 g quinoa, rinsed
* 4 (115 g) frozen skinless salmon fillets
* 1 tsp. sea salt, divided
* 1 tsp. freshly ground black pepper, divided
* 1 tbsp. extra-virgin olive oil
* 225 g green beans
* ½ tbsp. brown sugar
* 115 g unsalted butter, melted
* 2 garlic cloves, minced
* ½ tbsp. freshly squeezed lemon juice
* ½ tsp. dried thyme
* ½ tsp. dried rosemary

DIRECTIONS:

1. In the pot, add the water and quinoa and stir to combine. Place the Reversible Rack in the pot.
2. Put the salmon fillets on the rack.
3. Move the slider to PRESSURE. Close the lid, then turn the pressure release valve to SEAL position. Set the time to 2 minutes, press Start/Stop.
4. Meanwhile, add ½ tsp. of salt, ½ tsp. of black pepper, the olive oil and green beans into a medium bowl, toss well. Add the remaining ½ tsp. each of salt and black pepper, the brown sugar, butter, garlic, lemon juice, thyme, and rosemary in a small bowl mix them together.
5. After pressure cooking the rice and salmon is finish, move the pressure release valve to the Vent position to quick release the pressure. Remove the lid when the pressure has finished releasing carefully.
6. Use a kitchen towel to gently pat dry the salmon, then coat with the garlic butter sauce.
7. Arrange around the salmon with the green beans. Move slider to Air Fry/Hob, then select steam. Set the time to 7 minutes, then select Start/Stop to begin.
8. After cooking is finish, remove the salmon from the rack and serve with the rice and green beans.

CORN CHOWDER WITH SPICY PRAWN AND BACON

Prep Time: 10 minutes, Cook Time: 35 minutes, Serves: 4

INGREDIENTS:

* 4 tbsps. minced garlic, divided
* 4 rashers of bacon, chopped
* 1 onion, diced
* 450 g frozen corn
* 2 waxy potatoes, chopped
* 1 tsp. dried thyme
* 500 ml vegetable broth
* 1 tsp. sea salt, divided
* 1 tsp. freshly ground black pepper, divided
* 1 tbsp. extra-virgin olive oil
* ½ tsp. red pepper flakes
* 16 jumbo prawn, fresh or defrosted from frozen, peeled and deveined
* 180 ml double cream

DIRECTIONS:

1. Move the slider to Air Fry/Hob, then select Sear/Sauté. Preheat the Ninja Foodi for 5 minutes. Press Start/Stop.
2. In the preheated pot, add 2 tbsps. of garlic, the bacon and onion. Cook for 5 minutes, stirring occasionally. Reserve some of the bacon for garnish.
3. Stir in the corn, potatoes, thyme, vegetable broth, ½ tsp. of salt, and ½ tsp. of black pepper to the pot.
4. Move the slider to PRESSURE. Close the lid, then turn the pressure release valve to SEAL position. Set the time to 10 minutes, then press Start/Stop.
5. Meanwhile, add the remaining 2 tbsps. of garlic, ½ tsp. of salt, ½ tsp. of black pepper, the olive oil, red pepper flakes and prawn into a medium mixing bowl, toss well.
6. After pressure cooking the chowder is finish, move the pressure release valve to the Vent position to quick release the pressure. Remove the lid when the pressure has finished releasing carefully.
7. Stir the cream into the chowder. Put the Reversible Rack inside the pot over the chowder. Put the prawn on the rack.
8. Move slider to Air Fry/Hob, select BAKE. Set the time to 8 minutes. Press Start/Stop to begin.
9. After cooking is finish, remove the rack from the pot. Ladle into bowls with the corn chowder and top with the reserved bacon and prawn. Serve hot.

MEDITERRANEAN FISH STEW

Prep Time: 15 minutes, Cook Time: 20 minutes, Serves: 4 to 6

INGREDIENTS:

- 680 g skinless swordfish steak, cut into 2½-cm pieces
- 2 tbsps. extra-virgin olive oil
- 2 onions, chopped fine
- 1 tsp. coarse salt
- ½ tsp. pepper
- 1 tsp. minced fresh thyme or ¼ tsp. dried
- Pinch red pepper flakes
- 4 garlic cloves, minced, divided
- 800 g tinned whole peeled tomatoes, drained with juice reserved, chopped coarse
- 225 ml clam juice
- 60 ml dry white wine
- 30 g sultanas
- 2 tbsps. capers, rinsed
- 30 g pine nuts, toasted
- 10 g minced fresh mint
- 1 tsp. grated orange zest

DIRECTIONS:

1. Move slider to Air Fry/Hob, then select Sear/Sauté. Heat oil in the pot until shimmering. Add onions, salt, and pepper and cook about 5 minutes until onions are softened. Stir in pepper flakes, thyme, and 3/4 garlic and cook about 30 seconds until fragrant. Stir in tomatoes and reserved juice, wine, clam juice, sultanas, and capers. Nestle swordfish into pot and spoon cooking liquid over top.
2. Move the slider to PRESSURE. Close the lid. Then turn the pressure release valve to SEAL position. Cook for 1 minute. Turn off and quick-release pressure. Carefully remove lid, letting steam escape away from you.
3. Combine pine nuts, orange zest, mint, and remaining garlic in bowl. Season stew with salt and pepper. Sprinkle each portion with pine nut mixture and serve.

PHO WITH PRAWN

Prep Time: 10 minutes, Cook Time: 36 minutes, Serves: 6

INGREDIENTS:

- 400 g rice noodles, cooked according to the package directions
- 1 onion, peeled and halved
- 2 tbsps. rapeseed oil
- 1 (5-cm) piece fresh ginger, peeled
- 1½ tbsps. Chinese five-spice powder
- 2 tbsps. brown sugar
- 2 tbsps. coarse salt
- 1 L beef bone broth
- 60 ml fish sauce
- 2 L water
- 450 g peeled cooked prawn

DIRECTIONS:

1. Move slider to Air Fry/Hob, then select Sear/Sauté. Preheat the Ninja Foodi for 5 minutes.
2. Add oil, onion and ginger, sear on all sides for 6 minutes. Press Start/Stop to end.
3. Stir with the sugar, salt, five-spice powder, fish sauce, bone broth, and water for 1 minute.
4. Move the slider to PRESSURE. Close the lid, then turn the pressure release valve to SEAL position. Set the time to 30 minutes.
5. After cooking is complete, move pressure release valve to VENT position to quickly release the pressure. Carefully remove lid.
6. Take a bowl, add the desired amount of noodles to it. Top with 5 or 6 prawn and some sliced onion. Ladle the pho broth to cover the noodles, prawn, and onion.

SALMON CUSTARD

Prep Time: 10 minutes, Cook Time: 40 minutes, Serves: 4

INGREDIENTS:

* 450 g waxy potatoes (3 or 4 medium potatoes), peeled and cut into ½-cm slices
* ¾ tsp. coarse salt (or a scant ½ tsp. fine salt), divided
* 160 ml whole milk
* 3 large eggs
* 120 ml double cream
* ¼ tsp. freshly ground black pepper, plus more for finishing
* 3 tbsps. melted unsalted butter, divided
* 175 g smoked salmon, cut into chunks
* 3 tbsps. chopped fresh dill, divided

DIRECTIONS:

1. In the Foodi inner pot, add 250 ml of water. Put the potato slices on the Reversible Rack, or in a steaming basket, and place the rack in the pot in the lower position.
2. Move the slider to PRESSURE. Close the lid, then turn the pressure release valve to SEAL position. Adjust the cook time to 3 minutes. Press Start/Stop.
3. After cooking, quick release the pressure. Open and remove the Pressure Lid carefully. Take the rack out, sprinkle ¼ tsp. of coarse salt (or ⅛ tsp. of fine salt) over the potatoes, and allow them to cool. Empty the water out of the pot.
4. While the potatoes cook and cool, whisk the milk, eggs, remaining ½ tsp. of coarse salt (or ⅜ tsp. of fine salt), double cream and the pepper in a large bowl.
5. Use 2 tsps. or so of melted butter to grease a 1-litre, high-sided, round dish. Lay one-third of the potatoes on the base of the dish, spread with half the salmon, and sprinkle with 1 tbsp. of dill. Place another third of the potatoes over, and cover with the remaining salmon spread, 1 tbsp. of dill followed by the remaining third of the potatoes. Pour over with the custard, it should come up just to the top layer of potatoes but not cover them. (You may not need all the custard.)
6. In the pot, add 250 ml of water. Put the Reversible Rack in the pot in the lower position and put the baking dish on top.
7. Move the slider to PRESSURE. Close the lid, then turn the pressure release valve to the SEAL position. Adjust the cook time to 15 minutes. Press Start/Stop.
8. When the cooking is complete, naturally release the pressure for 10 minutes, then quick release any remaining pressure. Open and remove the Pressure Lid carefully.
9. Take the baking dish and rack out from the pot and pour the water out of the pot. Place the pot back to the base and place the rack back in the pot. Move slider to Air Fry/Hob, select BAKE. Adjust the time to 2 minutes to preheat. Press Start/Stop.
10. Meanwhile, drizzle over the top of the potatoes with the remaining melted butter. Open the Lid and place the dish on the rack. Close the lid, select BAKE, and set the cook time to 5 minutes. Press Start/Stop.
11. After broiling, open the lid and carefully remove the custard. Allow to cool for a few minutes. Sprinkle with the remaining 1 tbsp. of dill and season with additional pepper as desired.

SEAFOOD PAELLA

Prep Time: 10 minutes, Cook Time: 30 minutes, Serves: 4

INGREDIENTS:

* 1 tbsp. extra-virgin olive oil
* 450 g chorizo, cut into 1-cm slices
* 4 garlic cloves, minced
* 1 yellow onion, chopped
* 120 ml dry white wine
* 1 L chicken broth
* 400 g long-grain white rice
* ½ tsp. sea salt
* 1 tsp. turmeric
* 1½ tsps. smoked paprika
* ½ tsp. freshly ground black pepper
* 450 g small clams, scrubbed
* 450 g fresh prawn, peeled and deveined
* 1 red pepper, diced

DIRECTIONS:

1. Move slider to Air Fry/Hob, then select Sear/Sauté. Preheat the pot for 5 minutes.
2. In the preheated pot, add the oil and chorizo, cook for 3 minutes, until the meat is brown on both sides, stirring occasionally. Remove the chorizo from the pot and set aside.
3. Add the garlic and onion to the pot. Cook for 5 minutes, stirring occasionally. Add the wine and use a wooden spoon to stir, scraping up any brown bits from the bottom of the pot, and cook until the wine is reduced by half, about 2 minutes.
4. Add the broth and rice to the pot. Season with the salt, turmeric, paprika, and pepper.
5. Move the slider to PRESSURE. Close the lid, then turn the pressure release valve to SEAL position. Set the time to 5 minutes, then press Start/Stop.
6. After pressure cooking is finish, set the pressure release valve to Vent, to quick release the pressure. Remove the lid when the pressure has finished releasing carefully.
7. Move slider to Air Fry/Hob, then select Sear/Sauté. Add the clams and prawn to the pot. Press Start/ Stop to begin.
8. Cook until the prawn are pink and opaque and the clams have opened, about 6 minutes. Discard any unopened clams.
9. Place the chorizo back to the pot and add the red pepper. Stir to combine and serve immediately.

PRAWN AND MIXED VEGETABLE EGG ROLLS

Prep Time: 10 minutes, Cook Time: 30 minutes, Serves: 4

INGREDIENTS:

* 2 tsps. rice vinegar
* 1 tbsp. dry sherry
* 2 tbsps. soya sauce
* 2 tsps. sesame oil
* 2 garlic cloves, minced
* 1 tsp. grated peeled fresh ginger
* 1 large carrot, peeled and shredded
* 250 g shredded cabbage or coleslaw mix
* 1 tsp. sugar
* 3 spring onions, chopped
* 225 g prawn, peeled and coarsely chopped
* 100 g Sautéed Mushrooms, coarsely chopped
* ¼ tsp. freshly ground black pepper
* 1 tsp. cornflour
* 1 tbsp. water
* 8 to 10 egg roll wrappers
* Non-stick cooking spray, for cooking the egg rolls
* plum sauce or Chinese mustard for serving

DIRECTIONS:

1. Combine the rice vinegar, sherry and soya sauce in the Foodi pot. Then add the sesame oil, garlic, ginger, carrot, cabbage, sugar and spring onions to the pot.
2. Move the slider to PRESSURE. Close the lid, then turn the pressure release valve to the SEAL position. Set the cook time to 2 minutes. Press Start/Stop.
3. When the cooking is complete, quick release the pressure. Open and remove the Pressure Lid carefully.
4. Add the prawn, mushrooms and pepper to the pot. Move slider to Air Fry/Hob, then select Sear/Sauté. Bring the mixture to a simmer to cook the prawn and warm the mushrooms. Continue simmering until most of the liquid has evaporated, about 5 minutes. Place the filling into a bowl and set aside to cool. Wipe out the pot and place it back to the base.
5. To form the egg rolls, stir together the cornflour and water in a small bowl. Lay a wrapper on your work surface positioned with a corner pointed toward you. Use the cornflour mixture to lightly moisten the edges of the wrapper. Scoop 60 ml of filling just below the centre of the wrapper with a slotted spoon. As you scoop the filling out, leave as much liquid behind as possible. You want the rolls to be dry inside, not soggy.
6. Fold the bottom corner of the wrapper over the filling and tuck it under the filling. Roll once and then fold both sides in. Continue to roll up tightly. Repeat with the remaining wrappers and filling on the other side.
7. Move slider to Air Fry/Hob, select BAKE. Adjust the temperature to 200°C and the time to 5 minutes. Press Start/Stop.
8. Place 6 to 8 egg rolls in the Basket and use the cooking spray to spray. Turn them over and spray the other sides. Once the pot has preheated, place the basket in the pot.
9. Close the Lid and select BAKE. Adjust the temperature to 200°C and the cook time to 15 minutes. Press Start. After 6 minutes, open the lid and check the egg rolls. They should be crisp on top and golden brown. If not, close the lid and cook for another 1 to 2 minutes. Turn the rolls when the tops are crisp and cook for another 5 to 6 minutes or until crisp on the other side.
10. Repeat with any uncooked egg rolls. Allow the rolls to cool on a wire rack for 8 to 10 minutes, as the interiors will be very hot. Serve with plum sauce or Chinese mustard as desired.

TERIYAKI SALMON WITH PEA AND MUSHROOM

Prep Time: 10 minutes, Cook Time: 15 minutes, Serves: 4

INGREDIENTS:

* ½ tsp. coarse salt (or ¼ tsp. fine salt)
* 4 (145 g) skin-on salmon fillets
* ½ medium red pepper, cut into chunks
* 150 g snow peas or snap peas
* 80 ml Teriyaki Sauce, plus 1 tbsp.
* 60 ml water
* 100 g Sautéed Mushrooms
* 2 spring onions, chopped

DIRECTIONS:

1. Sprinkle the salt over the salmon fillets and place them on the Reversible Rack set in the upper position.
2. In the Foodi pot, add the red pepper and snow peas. Drizzle with 1 tbsp. of teriyaki sauce and pour in the water. Place the rack with the salmon in the pot.
3. Move the slider to PRESSURE. Close the lid, then turn the pressure release valve to SEAL position. Adjust the cook time to 1 minute. Press Start/Stop.
4. When the cooking is complete, quick release the pressure. Open and remove the Pressure Lid carefully.
5. Brush over the salmon with about half the remaining 80 ml of teriyaki sauce.
6. Move slider to Air Fry/Hob, select BAKE. Adjust the cook time to 7 minutes. Press Start/Stop. After cooking for 5 minutes, check the salmon. It should just flake apart when done. Cook for the remaining 2 minutes if needed.
7. After cooking, remove the rack with the salmon and set aside.
8. Add the mushrooms and spring onions to the vegetables in the pot and stir to heat through. If the sauce is too thin, move slider to Air Fry/Hob and select Sear/Sauté. Press Start/Stop. Simmer until the sauce reaches your consistency. Divide the vegetables among four plates and place the salmon on top, drizzle over with the remaining teriyaki sauce.

CHAPTER 8 SNACK AND DESSERT

CHEESY GARLIC PEA ARANCINI

Prep Time: 15 minutes, Cook Time: 45 minutes, Serves: 6

INGREDIENTS:

* 120 ml extra-virgin olive oil, plus 1 tbsp.
* 1 small yellow onion, diced
* 2 garlic cloves, minced
* 120 ml white wine
* 1¼ L chicken broth
* 400 g arborio rice
* 150 g frozen peas
* 175 g grated Parmesan cheese, plus more for garnish
* 1 tsp. freshly ground black pepper
* 1 tsp. sea salt
* 200 g fresh bread crumbs
* 2 large eggs

DIRECTIONS:

1. Move the slider to Air Fry/Hob, select Sear/Sauté. Preheat for 5 minutes.
2. In the preheated pot, add 1 tbsp. of oil and the onion. Cook until soft and translucent, stirring occasionally. Stir in the garlic and cook for 1 minute.
3. Place the wine, broth, and rice into the pot, stir to incorporate.
4. Move the slider to PRESSURE. Close the lid, then turn the pressure release valve to SEAL position. Set the time to 7 minutes. Press Start/Stop to begin.
5. After pressure cooking is finish, naturally release the pressure for 10 minutes, then turn the pressure release valve to the Vent position to quick release any remaining pressure. Remove the lid when the unit has finished releasing pressure carefully.
6. Add the frozen peas, Parmesan cheese, pepper and salt. Stir vigorously until the rice begins to thicken. Transfer the risotto to a large mixing bowl and allow it to cool.
7. At the same time, clean the pot. Stir together the bread crumbs and the remaining 120 ml of olive oil in a medium mixing bowl. Lightly beat the eggs in another mixing bowl.
8. Divide the risotto into 12 equal portions and shape each one into a ball. Dip each risotto ball in the beaten eggs, then dredge in the bread crumb mixture to coat well.
9. Arrange half of the arancini in the Cook & Crisp Basket in a single layer.
10. Move slider to Air Fry/Hob, select BAKE. Cook at 205°C for 10 minutes. Select Start/Stop to begin.
11. Repeat steps 9 and 10 to cook another half of arancini.

FRIED CRISPY DUMPLINGS

Prep Time: 20 minutes, Cook Time: 12 minutes, Serves: 8

INGREDIENTS:

* 1 large egg, beaten
* 225 g minced pork
* 20 g shredded Napa cabbage
* 1 carrot, shredded
* 2 tbsps. reduced-sodium soya sauce
* 1 garlic clove, minced
* ½ tbsp. grated fresh ginger
* ½ tbsp. sesame oil
* ½ tsp. sea salt
* ½ tsp. freshly ground black pepper
* 20 wonton wrappers
* 2 tbsps. sunflower oil

DIRECTIONS:

1. Put the Cook & Crisp Basket in the pot. Move slider to Air Fry/Hob, select Air Fry. set the temperature to 205°C, and set the time to 5 minutes to preheat the unit.
2. While preheating, combine the egg, pork, cabbage, carrot, soya sauce, garlic, ginger, sesame oil, salt, and pepper in a large mixing bowl.
3. On a clean work surface, place the wonton wrappers and spoon 1 tbsp. of the pork mixture into the centre of each wrapper. Use water to gently rub the edges of the wrappers. Fold the dough over the filling to create a half-moon shape, pinching the edges to seal. Use the sunflower oil to brush the dumplings.
4. Put the dumplings in the Cook & Crisp Basket. Select Air Fry, set the temperature to 205°C, and set the time to 12 minutes. Select Start/Stop to begin.
5. Six minutes later, open the lid, lift the basket and shake the dumplings. Lower the basket back into the pot and close the lid to resume cooking until achieve your desired crispiness.

LOADED SMASHED POTATOES WITH BACON

Prep Time: 10 minutes, Cook Time: 30 minutes, Serves: 4

INGREDIENTS:

* 350 g baby waxy potatoes
* 1 tsp. extra-virgin olive oil
* 30 g shredded Cheddar cheese
* 60 ml soured cream
* 2 slices streaky bacon, cooked and crumbled
* 1 tbsp. chopped fresh chives
* Sea salt

DIRECTIONS:

1. Put the Crisp Basket in the pot. Move slider to Air Fry/Hob, select Air Fry. Set the temperature to 180°C, and set the time to 5 minutes to preheat the unit.
2. While preheating, toss the potatoes with the oil until evenly coated.
3. After the pot and basket are preheated, open the lid and place the potatoes into the basket. Close the lid, select Air Fry. Set the temperature to 180°C, and set the time to 30 minutes. Press Start/Stop to begin.
4. 15 minutes later, open the lid, lift out the basket and shake the potatoes. Lower the basket back into the pot and close the lid to resume cooking.
5. After another 15 minutes, check the potatoes for your desired crispiness.
6. Take the potatoes out from the basket. Lightly crush the potatoes to split them with a large spoon. Top with the cheese, soured cream, bacon, and chives, and season with salt.

GARLIC-JICAMA CHIPS WITH SCALLION CASHEW DIP

Prep Time: 10 minutes, Cook Time: 40 minutes, Serves: 2

INGREDIENTS:

For The Jicama Chips:

* ½ jicama, peeled and cut into 32 (½-cm-thick) sticks
* 1 tbsp. avocado oil
* ¼ tsp. garlic powder
* ¼ to ½ tsp. chipotle powder
* ¼ to ½ tsp. sea salt
* ¼ tsp. freshly ground black pepper

For The Scallion Dip:

* 60 g roughly chopped spring onions
* 180 g raw cashews
* 120 ml coconut milk (boxed)
* 1 tbsp. apple cider vinegar
* 1 tbsp. freshly squeezed lemon juice
* 60 ml vegetable broth
* 1 garlic clove
* ½ tsp. sea salt

DIRECTIONS:

1. Use greaseproof paper to line the inner pot.

TO PREPARE THE JICAMA CHIPS:

1. Place the jicama sticks in a medium bowl, toss with the avocado oil to coat.
2. Add the garlic powder, chipotle powder, salt, and pepper, and toss again to coat. Adjust the seasonings, if needed.
3. Place the jicama sticks onto the pot. and spread in a single layer.
4. Move slider to Air Fry/Hob, select BAKE and cook at 205°C for 20 minutes, flip them over, and bake for another 15 to 20 minutes.

TO PREPARE THE SCALLION DIP:

1. While the jicama sticks bake, add all of the scallion dip ingredients into a high-speed blender, blend them together until creamy and smooth. Adjust the seasonings, if needed, and serve.

HEALTHY CRACKERS WITH SESAME SEEDS

Prep Time: 20 minutes, Cook Time: 30 minutes, Serves: 50 crackers

INGREDIENTS:

* 135 g of spelt flour
* 70 g of rye flour
* 2 tsps. of sesame seed
* 1 tsp. of agave syrup
* 1 tsp. of pure sea salt
* 180 ml of spring water
* 2 tbsps. of grape seed oil

DIRECTIONS:

1. In a medium bowl, combine all of the ingredients except the oil and mix well.
2. Make a dough ball. Add more flour if it is too liquid.
3. Prepare a place for rolling out the dough and use a piece of greaseproof paper to cover.
4. Use the grape seed oil to lightly grease the paper and place the dough on it.
5. Use a rolling pin to roll out the dough, adding more flour to avoid sticking.
6. Cut the dough into squares with a shape cutter. If you don't have a shape cutter, you can use a pizza cutter.
7. Place the squares on Cook & Crisp Basket and use a fork or a skewer to poke holes in each square.
8. Use a little grape seed oil to brush the dough and sprinkle with more pure sea salt if needed.
9. Move slider to Air Fry/Hob, select BAKE and cook at 180°C for 12 to 15 minutes or until the crackers are starting to become golden.
10. After baking, let cool before serving.

COCONUT CHOCOLATE AND DATE BISCUITS

Prep Time: 30 minutes, Cook Time: 5 minutes, Serves: 12

INGREDIENTS:

For The Biscuit Base:

* 70 g dried shredded unsweetened coconut
* 2 pinches sea salt
* 120 g raw almonds
* 1 packet stevia
* 2½ tbsps. coconut oil, melted

For the coconut caramel layer

* 35 g dried shredded unsweetened coconut
* 2 tbsps. coconut oil, melted
* 8 Medjool dates
* 1 tbsp. water, plus additional as needed
* Pinch sea salt

For The Chocolate Icing:

* 4 tbsps. coconut oil, melted
* 4 tbsps. unsweetened Dutch-processed cocoa powder
* 1 packet stevia

DIRECTIONS:

TO MAKE THE BISCUIT BASE:

1. Use greaseproof paper to line the pot.
2. Add the coconut into a food processor, blend for 60 seconds. Add the salt and almonds, blend until they are ground into a meal. Add the stevia and coconut oil, and blend until a dough form.
3. Roll the dough between two sheets of wax paper to a ½ cm thickness. Allow the dough to freeze for 10 minutes, or until firm.
4. Cut out 12 biscuits with a round biscuit cutter. Arrange each biscuit base on the inner pot.

TO MAKE THE COCONUT CARAMEL LAYER:

1. Spread the coconut in an even layer on Cook & Crisp Basket. Move slider to Air Fry/Hob, select BAKE and cook at 180°C for 5 minutes. Remove and cool.
2. Add the coconut oil, dates and water in a food processor. Blend to combine. Add the salt and more water, if needed. Continue to blend until the mixture resembles caramel. Add the toasted coconut and mix to combine.
3. Spread onto each biscuit base. with an equal layer of the caramel-coconut mixture.

TO MAKE THE CHOCOLATE ICING:

1. Mix together the coconut oil, cocoa powder and stevia in a small bowl.
2. Drizzle the icing over each of the 12 biscuits with a spoon.
3. Place the biscuits in the refrigerator to chill for 10 minutes to solidify the layers before eating.

VANILLA OAT APPLE CRISP

Prep Time: 10 minutes, Cook Time: 35 minutes, Serves: 6

INGREDIENTS:

* 175 ml apple juice
* 3 medium apples, cored and cut into ½-cm pieces
* 1 tsp. vanilla extract
* 1 tsp. ground cinnamon, divided
* 200 g rolled oats
* 60 ml maple syrup

DIRECTIONS:

1. Add the apple juice, apple slices, vanilla, and ½ tsp. of cinnamon in a large bowl. Mix well to thoroughly coat the apple slices.
2. Layer the apple slices on the bottom of the pot. Pour any leftover liquid over the apple slices.
3. Add the maple syrup, oats, and the remaining ½ tsp. of cinnamon in a large bowl, stir them together until the oats are completely coated.
4. Sprinkle over the apples with the oat mixture, make sure to evenly spread it out so that none of the apple slices are visible.
5. Move slider to Air Fry/Hob, select BAKE and cook at 190°C until the oats begin to turn golden brown, about 35 minutes, and serve.

SWEET BLUEBERRY AND CHIA SEED VANILLA COBBLER

Prep Time: 5 minutes, Cook Time: 45 minutes, Serves: 2 to 4

INGREDIENTS:

For The Blueberries:

* 150 g blueberries
* 2 tbsps. unrefined whole cane sugar
* 1 tbsp. chia seeds

For The Topping:

* 70 g oat flour
* 50 g almond flour
* 2 tbsps. coconut oil (melted/liquid)
* 4 tbsps. coconut milk (boxed)
* 1½ tsps. baking powder
* 1 tsp. vanilla bean powder
* 2 tbsps. unrefined whole cane sugar
* ¼ tsp. sea salt

DIRECTIONS:

TO PREPARE THE BLUEBERRIES:

1. Add the sugar, blueberries and chia seeds into a medium bowl, stir them together. Transfer the mixture to a 23 cm oval ovenproof baking dish or four (120 ml) ramekin bowls.

TO PREPARE THE TOPPING:

1. Combine all of the topping ingredients in the pot, stir them together until well combined.

TO ASSEMBLE:

1. Drop the topping over the blueberry mixture, a tablespoonful at a time. You can leave the topping as "dollops" or evenly spread it over the top of the blueberry mixture for a full crust.
2. Move slider to Air Fry/Hob, select BAKE. Cook at 180°C until the topping is slightly golden and cooked through, about 45 minutes.
3. After baking, serve warm.

DATES, SPELT AND SULTANA BISCUITS

Prep Time: 10 minutes, Cook Time: 18 minutes, Serves: 2

INGREDIENTS:

* 135 g spelt flour
* 125 g dates, pitted
* 1/16 tsp. sea salt
* 1¾ tbsps. rapeseed oil
* 40 g sultanas
* 3 ½ tbsps. applesauce homemade or pureed apples
* ⅔ tbsp. spring water
* 2 tbsps. agave syrup

DIRECTIONS:

1. In a food processor, add the flour, dates and salt, pulse until well blended.
2. Transfer the flour mixture into a medium bowl, add all of the remaining ingredients, and stir until well mixed.
3. Divide the mixture into parts, each part about 2 tbsps. of the mixture, and then form each part into a ball.
4. Arrange the biscuit balls on Cook & Crisp Basket lined with parchment sheet, use a fork to flatten it slightly. Move slider to Air Fry/Hob, select BAKE and cook at 180°C for 18 minutes until done.
5. After baking, allow the biscuits to cool for 10 minutes and serve.

NUTTY LEMON OATMEAL CACAO BISCUITS

Prep Time: 30 minutes, Cook Time: 35 minutes, Serves: 14 biscuits

INGREDIENTS:

* 12 pitted Medjool dates
* Boiling water, for soaking the dates
* 1 tbsp. freshly squeezed lemon juice
* 250 ml unsweetened applesauce
* 1 tsp. vanilla extract
* 1 tbsp. water, plus more as needed (optional)
* 125 g oat flour
* 150 g old-fashioned oats
* 2 tbsps. lemon zest
* 90 g coarsely chopped walnuts
* 1 tbsp. cacao powder
* ½ tsp. bread soda

DIRECTIONS:

1. Add the dates into a small bowl, cover with enough boiling water. Allow to sit for 15 to 20 minutes to soften.
2. Use greaseproof paper to line the pot.
3. Drain the excess liquid from the dates and place them into a blender, then add the lemon juice, applesauce, and vanilla. Puree until a thick paste form. If the mixture isn't getting smooth, add the water, 1 tbsp. at a time.
4. Add the oat flour, oats, lemon zest, walnuts, cacao powder, and bread soda in a large bowl, stir them together. Pour in the date mixture and stir to combine. One at a time, scoop 4 tbsp portions of dough, gently roll into a ball, and lightly press down in the inner pot. The biscuit is about 2½ cm thick and roughly 8 cm in diameter.
5. Move slider to Air Fry/Hob, select BAKE and cook at 150°C until the tops of the biscuits look crispy and dry, about 30 to 35 minutes. After baking, transfer to a wire rack to cool.
6. Keep in an airtight container at room temperature for up to 1 week.

CHAPTER 9 CLASSIC BRITISH FAVOURITES

STRESS-FREE FULL ENGLISH BREAKFAST

Prep Time: 10 minutes, Cook Time: 23 minutes, Serves: 1

INGREDIENTS:

* 2 sausages
* 2-3 rashers of bacon
* 1 flat mushrooms
* 1-2 ripe tomatoes
* 1 large egg
* 1 slice of bread
* 1 thick slice of black pudding

DIRECTIONS:

1. Move slider to Air Fry/Hob, select Air Fry.
2. Preheat the Ninja Foodi to 180°C for 5 minutes. Press Start/Stop.
3. Place sausages in the Cook & Crisp Basket in the pot and fry for 10 minutes, turning every 2-3 minutes.
4. Transfer sausages to a hot plate to keep warm.
5. Add the mushroom, pudding, and halved tomatoes to the basket. Air fry for about 6 minutes, turning at halfway point.
6. Fry bacon for 3 minutes until crispy.
7. Place eggs in the Basket and fry them to your liking.
8. Bake the bread in the Ninja Foodi until browned.
9. Transfer cooked foods to a plate and enjoy.

BEST HOMEMADE SCOTCH EGG

Prep Time: 10 minutes, Cook Time: 35 minutes, Serves: 4

INGREDIENTS:

* 1 egg, beaten
* 80 g plain flour
* 80 g panko bread crumbs
* 455 g sausage meat
* 4 hard-cooked eggs, peeled
* 1 tsp. dried onion powder
* 1 tsp. salt

DIRECTIONS:

1. Move slider to Air Fry/Hob, select Air Fry.
2. Preheat the Ninja Foodi to 200°C.
3. Combine pork sausage, onion and salt in a large bowl, and mix well. Shape mixture into 4 equal burgers.
4. Coat each hard-cooked egg with flour; place on sausage burger and shape sausage around egg.
5. Dip each into beaten egg; coat with bread crumbs to cover completely. Place on the Cook & Crisp Basket.
6. Air Fry for 25 minutes.
7. Remove from the pot and serve.

BEEF SHEPARD'S PIE

Prep Time: 20 minutes, Cook Time: 45 minutes, Serves: 5

INGREDIENTS:

* 1 L beef or chicken stock
* 120 ml milk
* 100 g butter
* 2 egg yolks
* 2 onions (peeled and diced)
* 2 large carrots (peeled and diced)
* 50 g butter
* sprigs thyme
* 500 g minced lamb
* 250 g frozen peas
* 500 g (to 600) potatoes (peeled and cut into chunks)
* 1 tbsp. tomato puree
* 1 tbsp. ketchup
* 2 tbsps. Worcestershire sauce
* 2 tbsps. olive oil

DIRECTIONS:

1. Move slider to Air Fry/Hob, select BAKE.
2. Preheat the Ninja Foodi to 190°C.
3. In a skillet, sauté the onions, carrots, oil, and butter until just starting to color.
4. Add the thyme and beef. Turn up the heat and sauté until browned.
5. Add in remaining ingredients up until the stock.
6. Cook for 18 minutes until the liquid has reduced.
7. Season and let stand for a few minutes.
8. Add the peas and then transfer to the basket.
9. Cook the potatoes until tender. Add the milk and the remaining ingredients.
10. Spread the potatoes on top of the meat.
11. Bake until the topping is golden brown.
12. Let it rest for 10 minutes to serve.

PROPER ENGLISH COTTAGE PIE

Prep Time: <5 minutes, Cook Time: 45 minutes, Serves: 4-5

INGREDIENTS:

* 450 g minced beef
* 1 tin of chopped tomatoes
* 1 medium onion, chopped
* 2 carrot, medium peeled and diced
* 100 g frozen peas
* 2 garlic cloves
* Veg, chicken or beef stock cube
* Gravy granules (enough to thicken)
* 600 ml water
* Potatoes (Not white) – 8 medium potatoes
* 25 g butter
* 50 ml milk or cream
* Salt and pepper to taste
* cooking spray

DIRECTIONS:

1. Move slider to Air Fry/Hob, then use the dial to select Air Fry.
2. Preheat the Ninja Foodi to 180ºC. and spray the Cook & Crisp Basket with oil.
3. Peel and chop the onion, garlic and carrots then heat the pot with about 2 tbsps. of oil.
4. Put the veg you just chopped into the pot and cook slowly without colouring until the onions are soft.
5. Peel the potatoes then make sure they are roughly the same size, add to the other pot then cover with cold water
6. Heat on high temperature until boiling then lower the heat, cover with a lid and simmer till cooked.
7. Add the mince and use a wooden to break it apart. Cook it until it has browned.
8. Add the chopped tomatoes and stir well then add the water and stock cube, stir then turn the heat right down and allow to simmer for 15 minutes.
9. Add the peas and cook for another 5 minutes.
10. Add 2 tbsps. gravy granules to the pot then stir well, you may need to add more as the dish shouldn't be watery at all.
11. Add the mince sauce to the Cook & Crisp basket, don't overfill.
12. Mash the potatoes then add the butter and milk or cream with ½ tsp. each of salt and pepper.
13. Spoon the mash on top of the mince mix in the basket then bake at 180□ for 20 minutes.
14. Remove from the pot and serve immediately.

THE CLASSIC STEAK AND KIDNEY PIE

Prep Time: 15 minutes, Cook Time: 1 hour, Serves: 8

INGREDIENTS:

* 1 roll of puff pastry
* 1 egg, beaten
* 2 sheep's kidneys, washed, skinned, halved, core removed, cut into 1.25 cm cubes
* 500 g stewing steak (blade, flank, skirt or round), cut into 2.5 cm cubes
* freshly ground black pepper
* 120 ml water
* 3 tbsps. plain flour
* 2 tbsps. olive oil
* 2 tbsps. parsley, finely chopped
* cooking spray
* 1 tsp. salt

DIRECTIONS:

1. Move slider to Air Fry/Hob, then use the dial to select "BAKE".
2. Preheat the Ninja Foodi to 220ºC and spray the basket with oil.
3. Put the flour, seasonings, steak, and kidney pieces into a plastic bag, shaking to combine well.
4. In a heavy pot, heat the oil and brown the meat, stirring constantly for about 5 minutes.
5. Add the water. Cover the lid and cook for at least one hour.
6. Allow it cool and mix in the parsley. Roll out the pastry until it is slightly larger than the lid of the pie dish.
7. Cut a strip about 2.5 cm wide and place it around the dampened rim of the dish. Brush with cold water and transfer the steak and kidney mixture to the dish, then cover with the remaining pastry, pressing into the pastry rim to seal.
8. Press a pattern around the edge of the pie using a knife end and glaze with the egg, make a hole in the middle so that the steam can escape.
9. Place it in the basket and bake for 18 minutes, then set the temperature to 180°C and cook for a further 20minutes.
10. Remove from the pot and enjoy.

EASY YORKSHIRE PUDDING

Prep Time: 20 minutes, Cook Time: 25 minutes, Serves: 6

INGREDIENTS:

- 100 g plain flour
- ¼ tsp. salt
- 3 large free-range eggs
- 225 ml milk
- 4 tbsps. sunflower oil

DIRECTIONS:

1. Move slider to Air Fry/Hob, then use the dial to select "BAKE".
2. Preheat the Ninja Foodi to 220ºC.
3. In a bowl, mix together the flour and salt. Make a hole in the middle and add the eggs and a little milk.
4. Whisk until smooth, then gradually add the remaining milk.
5. Pour the mixture into a jug.
6. Measure a tsp. of oil into each hole of a 12-bun tray.
7. Place in the basket and bake for 5 minutes.
8. Lift out the basket and pour the batter equally between the holes. Return the batter quickly to the pot and cook for a further 20 minutes.
9. Serve hot.

AUTHENTIC CORNISH PASTIES

Prep Time: 20 minutes, Cook Time: 45 minutes, Serves: 6

INGREDIENTS:

- cooking spray
- 1 roll of ready-made shortcrust pastry

For The Cornish Pasty Filling:

- 450 g potato, finely diced
- 150 g turnip, finely diced
- 150 g onion, finely chopped
- 300 g beef skirt, finely chopped
- Salt and black pepper
- 1 tbsp. plain flour
- 40 g butter
- 1 egg, beaten

DIRECTIONS:

1. Move slider to Air Fry/Hob, select BAKE.
2. Preheat the Ninja Foodi to 180ºC and spay the basket with oil.
3. Roll out the pastry.
4. Cut out 6 discs of pastry.
5. Sprinkle the vegetables separately with salt and black pepper.
6. In a bowl, mix beef with the flour and some salt and pepper. Place some potatoes, turnip, onions, and beef on one half of the circle, leaving a gap around the edge. Dot with butter.
7. Brush around the perimeter of the pastry circle with the beaten egg, then fold the pastry over the vegetables and meat and seal firmly. Starting at one side, roll up the edges to form a sealed D-shaped pasty.
8. Brush the whole pasty with a beaten egg, then use a sharp knife to make a hole in the middle so that the steam can escape.
9. Repeat to make the other pasties.
10. Put the pasties in the basket and bake for 40 minutes.
11. Let them rest for 5 -10 minutes to serve.

LANCASHIRE LAMB HOTPOT

Prep Time: 20 minutes, Cook Time: 2 hours 30 minutes, Serves: 4

INGREDIENTS:

- 900 g boneless lamb rib or shoulder, cut into 4-cm pieces
- 2 large onions, peeled and sliced
- 680 g potatoes, peeled and sliced
- 350 ml lamb stock
- 2 bay leaves
- Salt and black pepper
- 1 tsp. dried thyme
- Sunflower oil or melted butter, for glazing

DIRECTIONS:

1. Move slider to Air Fry/Hob, select "BAKE"
2. Preheat the Ninja Foodi to 170ºC.
3. Add the lamb to a large ovenproof casserole dish.
4. Sprinkle with salt, pepper, thyme and bay leaves. Add the onions, then place the potatoes on top in overlapping layers.
5. Pour the stock into the dish. Coat the top of the potatoes with oil.
6. Place the dish in the Ninja Foodi pot and bake for 2 hours.
7. Set the temperature to 200°C and bake for a further 25 minutes.
8. Serve hot.

BANGERS AND MASH WITH ONION GRAVY

Prep Time: <5 minutes, Cook Time: 10 minutes, Serves: 8

INGREDIENTS:

* 6 large potatoes
* 8 sausages
* 1 medium onion, thinly sliced
* 590 ml beef stock
* 1 tbsp. plain flour
* 25 g butter
* 1 tbsp. cooking oil
* cooking spray

DIRECTIONS:

1. Move slider to Air Fry/Hob and preheat the Ninja Foodi to 200°C.
2. Peel the potatoes and boil them.
3. Heat ½ tbsp. of cooking oil in a large saucepan. Add the sliced onions and sauté until they are browned.
4. Coat the onions with the plain flour.
5. Gradually add the stock and bring it to a boil. Cook gently for 5-10 minutes.
6. Place the sausages in the basket and air fry for 3 minutes per side.
7. Mash potatoes with butter plus a little salt and pepper.
8. Transfer mashed potatoes to a plate, top with sausages, and spoon over the gravy. Serve immediately.

CRISPY FISH AND CHIPS

Prep Time: 15 minutes, Cook Time: 30 minutes, Serves: 4

INGREDIENTS:

* cooking spray
* 4 fillets of cod (200 g per person)

For the Batter:

* 250 g plain flour
* 50 g corn flour
* 1 L bottle of sparkling water
* 1 tsp. sea salt

For the Chips:

* 6 large potatoes

DIRECTIONS:

1. Move slider to Air Fry/Hob, select Air Fry.
2. Preheat the Ninja Foodi to 150°C and coat the cook & crisp basket with oil.
3. Prepare the batter and put it in the refrigerator for about twenty minutes.
4. In a large bowl, combine the 225 g flour, the corn flour and the salt and mix gently.
5. Add the sparkling water little by little while stirring gently with a whisk. If it's too watery add a little flour if it's too stodgy add a little water.
6. You don't need to whisk it perfectly as some lumps of flour will add to the crunch once cooked. Chill in the refrigerator for 20 minutes.
7. Peel the potatoes and cut into thin slices. Rinse in cold water and use a tea towel to dry it thoroughly. Place the chips in the basket.
8. Air Fry the chips for 5 minutes.
9. Cut the fish fillets into smaller pieces of roughly equal size.
10. Adjust the temperature to 190°C.
11. Add a pinch of sea salt to the remaining flour. Dip your pieces of fish in the flour. Shake off the excess flour and dip in the batter.
12. Fry the fish for 5 minutes, shaking the basket halfway.
13. Take one of the pieces out and break one of the pieces to check if it's cooked.
14. Put chips in the Ninja Foodi for a further 2 minutes to brown up and get crispy.
15. Remove from the pot and use kitchen paper to take off any excess oil.

BRITISH-STYLE PIG IN BLANKETS

Prep Time: <5 minutes, Cook Time: 15-20 minutes, Serves: 4-6

INGREDIENTS:

* 12 rashers
* 12 pork sausages
* 1 tbsp. clear honey
* ½ tbsp. grainy mustard
* 1 tbsp. chopped rosemary

DIRECTIONS:

1. Move slider to Air Fry/Hob, then use the dial to select Air Fry.
2. Preheat the Ninja Foodi to 180°C and cover the cook & crisp basket with foil.
3. Wrap a rasher around each sausage and put on the basket. Gently heat the honey, grainy mustard and chopped rosemary in a small pan until they bubble.
4. Brush the mixture over the sausages and air fry for 15 minutes. Sprinkle a little more chopped rosemary on top for garnish before serving.

ROAST BEEF WITH CARROTS AND ONIONS

Prep Time: <5 minutes, Cook Time: 1 hour-1 hour 20 minutes, Serves: 5-6

INGREDIENTS:

* 900 g beef roasting joint
* 2 carrots, diced
* 2 onions, diced
* cooking spray

DIRECTIONS:

1. Move slider to Air Fry/Hob, then use the dial to select Air Fry.
2. Preheat the Ninja Foodi to 180°C and coat the basket with oil.
3. Put the diced carrots and onions in the baske
4. Place the beef joint on top of the vegetables.
5. Season the beef and cover loosely with tinfoil.
6. Air fry for 1 hour 10 minutes.
7. Remove from the pot and serve.

SUNDAY ROAST BEEF AND GRAVY

Prep Time: 30 minutes, Cook Time: 1 hour 30 minutes, Serves: 4

INGREDIENTS:

For The Potatoes:

* 900 g potatoes, peeled and cut into bite-size chunks
* 2 garlic bulbs, halved widthways
* 2 tbsps. sunflower oil

For The Yorkshire Puddings:

* 75 g plain flour
* 1 large egg
* 75 ml milk
* 4 tsps. sunflower oil

For The Vegetables:

* 200 g Chantenay carrots
* 400 g savoy cabbage, core removed, sliced
* 50 g butter
* cooking spray

For The Beef:

* 900 g beef roasting joint

For The Gravy:

* 100 ml red wine
* 300 ml beef stock
* 1 tbsp. brown sugar
* 1 tbsp. cornflour

DIRECTIONS:

1. Move slider to Air Fry/Hob, select Air Fry.
2. Preheat the Ninja Foodi to 180°C and spay the basket with oil.
3. Add the salted water and potatoes to a pan and bring it to a boil. Cook for 5 minutes, then drain.
4. Heat the oil in a skillet. Add the potatoes and garlic halves to the hot oil – turning them to coat. Place in the basket and air fry for 10 minutes.
5. Set the Ninja Foodi temperature to 160°C. Remove the potatoes and set aside, keeping warm. Season the beef joint and place in the basket.
6. Select BAKE. Cook for about 45 minutes for medium-rare, basting every 12 minutes.
7. Prepare the Yorkshire pudding batter. Sift the flour into a bowl and season with black pepper. Whisk together the egg, milk and 50 ml water in a jug. Make a hole in the flour and gradually pour in the egg mix, whisking until smooth.
8. To make the gravy. In a small saucepan, add the wine and sugar, and cook for 2-3 minutes. Add the stock and continue to reduce by a third. In a small cup, whisk together the cornflour and 1 tbsp. water, then stir it into the gravy to thicken.
9. Take out the beef and cover loosely with foil. Let it rest for a minimum of 15 minutes.
10. Spray the 8 holes of a fairy cake or muffin tin with the oil, then remove and carefully divide the Yorkshire pudding batter between each. Move slider to Air Fry/Hob, select BAKE. Set the temperature to 200°C and cook for 8 minutes.
11. Meanwhile, cook the carrots for 8-10 minutes until tender. Blanch the cabbage in boiling water for 2 minutes. Drain the vegetables and stir through the butter. Reheat the gravy over a medium-low heat if needed.
12. Carve the beef into thin slices with a sharp knife.
13. Transfer to warm serving plates. Serve the beef with the potatoes, Yorkshire puddings, carrots, cabbage and gravy.

HOMEMADE CHRISTMAS DINNER

Prep Time: 30 minutes, Cook Time: 1 hour 30 minutes, Serves: 4

INGREDIENTS:

* cooking spray
* 200 g brussels sprouts
* 40 g cranberry sauce
* 1 chicken stock cube
* 1 stuffed turkey joint
* 4 pigs in blankets
* 20 g wholegrain mustard
* 4 potatoes
* 20 g of pine nuts
* 160 g Chantenay carrots
* 10 g Marmite pot
* 25 g honey
* 3 garlic cloves
* 200 g parsnips

DIRECTIONS:

1. Move slider to Air Fry/Hob, select Air Fry.
2. Preheat the Ninja Foodi to 220ºC and spay the basket with oil.
3. In a pot, add the water and bring it to a boil. Peel and halve the potatoes, then add them to the pot with a large pinch of salt, cook on high for 10-15 minutes.
4. Peel and chop the parsnips into batons.
5. Trim and halve the Chantenay carrots (no need to peel!)
6. Drain the cooked potatoes in a colander and shake them until they're fluffy.
7. Place the parsnips and Chantenay carrots in the cook & crisp Basket with a drizzle of vegetable oil and a pinch of salt.
8. Top the turkey joint and pigs in blankets. Season the turkey with a pinch of salt and pepper.
9. Select Air Fry and fry for an initial 7-8 minutes.
10. Add the potatoes to the basket, spray with the oil and season with a pinch of salt.
11. Bake for 25 minutes.
12. Meanwhile, re-boil half pot of water.
13. Dissolve the chicken stock cube in 250 ml boiled water. Add the marmite and stir well.
14. Lower the pot to a medium-low heat and add 15 g butter.
15. Once melted, add 2 tsps. flour and cook for 30 seconds, stirring to form a paste
16. Add the stock to the pan and cook for 10-15 minutes.
17. Slice the Brussels sprouts into thirds, and peel and finely slice the garlic.
18. Heat a drizzle of olive oil in a large wide-based pan over a medium heat.
19. Once hot, add the sliced sprouts, a pinch of salt and pepper. Cook for 10 minutes and stir frequently.
20. In a bowl, mix the wholegrain mustard and honey.
21. Once the potatoes and turkey have had 20 minutes, remove from the pot and let them rest for a few minutes.
22. Drizzle the honey mustard glaze over the carrots and parsnips and return them to the Ninja Foodi with the potatoes for 8 minutes further.
23. Add the sliced garlic and pine nuts to the sprouts and cook for a further 2-3 minutes.
24. Warm up the gravy over a low heat.
25. Slice the rested turkey and serve with the pigs in blankets, roast potatoes, honey mustard veg and garlic & pine nut sprouts to the side. Add a dollop of cranberry sauce to the side and drizzle over the gravy.

SAGE AND ONION STUFFING

Prep Time: 10 minutes, Cook Time: 10 minutes, Serves: 6

INGREDIENTS:

* cooking spray
* 400 g breadcrumbs
* 200 g butter
* 1 medium to large onion
* 2 garlic cloves
* 5 tsps. dried sage
* ¼ tsp. salt and pepper

DIRECTIONS:

1. Move slider to Air Fry/Hob, then use the dial to select Air Fry.
2. Preheat the Ninja Foodi to 180ºC and spay the basket with oil.
3. Cut the onion and garlic as finely as you can.
4. Place the butter, onion, dried sage, and garlic in the basket and air fry for 3 minutes.
5. Season with salt and pepper, stir then add the breadcrumbs little by little.
6. Transfer to a bowl and stir well.

BEEF WELLINGTON WITH MIXED MUSHROOMS

Prep Time: 10 minutes, Cook Time: 35 minutes, Serves: 6

INGREDIENTS:

* 1 kg fillet of beef, well-trimmed
* 1 small onion, finely chopped
* 2 shallots, finely chopped
* 350 g mushrooms, finely chopped
* A pinch nutmeg
* 500 g roll of ready-made puff pastry
* 1 egg, beaten
* 75 g butter
* 1 tbsp. olive oil
* cooking spray
* Salt and ground black pepper

DIRECTIONS:

1. Move slider to Air Fry/Hob, select “BAKE”.
2. Preheat the air fryer to 230ºC and spray the basket with oil.
3. In a small pan, heat the oil and 50 g butter. Add the onion and shallots and cook until transparent.
4. Add the mushrooms, seasoning, and nutmeg. Heat over moderate heat and stir regularly until all moisture from the mushrooms has evaporated. Transfer to a plate to cool.
5. Heat the remaining butter. Season the beef then brown it on all sides. Allow to cool while you roll the pastry into an oblong shape, large enough to wrap around the beef.
6. Pour the cold mushroom mixture over the pastry, leaving a 2cm border all around. Moisten the edges with beaten egg. Place the cooled meat in the centre and wrap the pastry around it. Seal the edges and place on the basket, with the seal underneath. Brush the parcel with the beaten egg.
7. Put it in the refrigerator for 20 minutes to chill.
8. Bake for 10 minutes. Then set the temperature to 200°C and bake for a further 20 minutes. Cook for five minutes less if you like it rare.
9. Remove from the pot and serve.

CLASSIC ENGLISH TOAD-IN-THE HOLE

Prep Time: <5 minutes, Cook Time: 50 minutes, Serves: 12

INGREDIENTS:

* cooking spray

For The Batter:

* 100 g plain flour
* 2 eggs
* 150 ml semi-skimmed milk

For The Toad:

* 8 pork sausages
* 1 onion, finely sliced
* 1 tbsp. vegetable oil

For The Gravy:

* 1 onion, finely sliced
* 1 tbsp. vegetable oil
* 2 tsps. plain flour
* 2 tsps. English mustard
* 2 tsps. Worcestershire sauce
* 1 vegetable stock cube, made up to 300ml

DIRECTIONS:

1. Move slider to Air Fry/Hob, select BAKE.
2. Preheat the Ninja Foodi to 200ºC and spray the basket with oil.
3. In a bowl, combine the flour and eggs. Slowly mix in the milk then beat until smooth.
4. Put the sausages in the basket, scatter over the sliced onion and drizzle over the oil. Bake for 10 minutes.
5. Lift out the basket, pour the batter over and around the sausages then lower the basket back into the pot and cook for a further 25 minutes.
6. To make the gravy. Heat the oil in a saucepan and fry the remaining onion for 5 minutes. Sprinkle over the flour and cook, stirring until thickened. Add the mustard, Worcestershire sauce, and stock, stirring until smooth and thickened.
7. Pour the gravy over the toad in the hole and enjoy it.

BRITISH GAMMON STEAK, EGG AND CHIPS

Prep Time: <5 minutes, Cook Time: 46 minutes, Serves: 1

INGREDIENTS:

* 1 large baking potato, unpeeled, cut into chunky chips
* 1 small gammon steak
* 1 egg
* 1 tsp. olive oil
* cooking spray

DIRECTIONS:

1. Move slider to Air Fry/Hob, select BAKE.
2. Preheat the pot to 200°C and spay the basket with oil.
3. Sprinkle the potatoes with the oil, some salt and pepper. Put in the basket and bake for 20 minutes.
4. Lift out the basket and turn the chips.
5. Push to edges of the basket, put the gammon in the center and cook for a further 7 minutes. Turn the gammon over, then crack the egg into the corner of the tray.
6. Cook for 5 minutes more. Remove from the pot and serve.

CRISPY ONION RINGS

Prep Time: <5 minutes, Cook Time: 10 minutes, Serves: 12

INGREDIENTS:

* 120 g plain flour
* 40 g cornflour
* 1 large onion, sliced into rings
* 100 ml sparkling water
* ½ tsp. sea salt
* cooking spray

DIRECTIONS:

1. Move slider to Air Fry/Hob, then use the dial to select Air Fry.
2. Preheat the Ninja Foodi to 180°C and spay the basket with oil.
3. In a bowl, mix together 100 g of flour, cornflour, salt, pepper and sparkling water until smooth batter is achieved.
4. Dip the onion rings into the leftover flour.
5. Dip into batter and put it in the basket.
6. Air fry for 3-4 minutes until golden and crispy.
7. Serve immediately.

REAL WELSH RAREBIT

Prep Time: 10 minutes, Cook Time: 10 minutes, Serves: 6

INGREDIENTS:

* 350 g Mature Cheddar, grated
* 1 large egg, lightly beaten
* Pinch cayenne pepper
* 12 thick slices white bread
* 2 tbsps. beer (preferably stout)
* 1 tsp. Worcestershire sauce
* 1 tsp. English mustard
* cooking spray

DIRECTIONS:

1. Set aside 1 heaped tbsp. of grated cheese.
2. In a bowl, mix together the rest with the egg, beer, Worcestershire sauce, mustard and cayenne.
3. Move slider to Air Fry/Hob, select BAKE. Preheat the pot to 200°C and spay the basket with oil.
4. Put the bread in the basket and bake for 4 minutes on both sides.
5. Lift out the basket, scatter the cheese mixture over it and then sprinkle on the reserved cheese.
6. Lower the basket back into the pot and bake until the cheese is melted and starting to turn golden brown.
7. Remove from the pot and serve.

TASTY CULLEN SKINK

Prep Time: 30 minutes, Cook Time: 30 minutes, Serves: 2

INGREDIENTS:

* 25 g butter
* 1 medium onion
* 400 g potatoes
* 280 g smoked haddock (approximately 2 fillets)
* 300 ml whole milk
* 300 ml boiling water
* Optional – Parsley to garnish
* Cooking spray

DIRECTIONS:

1. Move slider to Air Fry/Hob, select Air Fry.
2. Preheat the Ninja Foodi to 180ºC and coat an ovenproof dish with oil.
3. Put the milk and smoked haddock skin-up into one pan and allow to sit. The milk should cover the whole fish.
4. Chop an onion as finely as you can. Peel and cube the potatoes.
5. Add the butter and onion to the pot and air fry for around 3 minutes.
6. Add the potatoes and cook for a minute before pouring in 300 ml of boiling water. Cover and allow to simmer for 15 minutes or so until the potatoes are cooked through.
7. Heat the milk and haddock gradually, moving the milk around with a wooden spoon every now and then so it doesn't stick. It should take about 10 minutes.
8. Use a slotted spoon to remove the smoked haddock from the milk and keep the milk to one side.
9. Allow the fish to cool slightly and any skin or bones and discard them.
10. Roughly mash about a quarter of the potatoes with a fork.
11. Add the milk to the dish of potatoes and onions and stir for a few minutes to combine.
12. Separate the smoked haddock into large chunks with a fork then add to the dish and stir gently through. Season with salt and pepper.
13. Add parsley for garnish and serve.

HEALTHY BUBBLE AND SQUEAK

Prep Time: 20 minutes, Cook Time: 25 minutes, Serves: 4

INGREDIENTS:

* 1 fresh egg, lightly beaten
* 150 g brussels sprouts, cooked and finely sliced
* 25 g butter
* 4 potatoes peeled, cooked and mashed
* 1 tbsp. olive oil
* 1 tbsp. milk
* 2 tbsps. plain flour
* 1 tsp. salt freshly ground

DIRECTIONS:

1. Add the potatoes to a pan and cover with cold water. Bring it to a boil, then cook for 15-20 minutes.
2. Strain the potatoes and add the butter and milk, mash well.
3. Add the sprouts, flour, and seasoning to the mashed potato, and pour in the beaten egg. Combine all the ingredients together and turn out on to a lightly floured surface.
4. Flatten the mixture with a rolling pin and use a scone cutter to cut the mixture.
5. Move slider to Air Fry/Hob, select Air Fry. Preheat the Ninja Foodi to 180ºC and coat the basket with oil.
6. Put the patty shapes in the basket and air fry on each side for 4 minutes.
7. Remove from the pot and enjoy.

CLASSIC VICTORIA SPONGE CAKE

Prep Time: 15 minutes, Cook Time: 25 minutes, Serves: 8

INGREDIENTS:

* 160 g unsalted butter, softened
* 160 g self-raising flour, sifted
* 160 g caster sugar
* 3 large eggs, lightly beaten
* 100 ml double cream
* 125 g strawberry jam
* 1 tsp. vanilla extract
* 1 tbsp. icing sugar, for dusting

DIRECTIONS:

1. Move slider to Air Fry/Hob and select STEAM BAKE. Preheat the pot to 150°C.
2. Grease and line 20cm springform cake tins with nonstick baking paper.
3. Stir the butter, vanilla extract, and sugar with an electric handheld whisk until light and fluffy.
4. Add the lightly beaten egg a tbsp. at a time, beating until fully incorporated.
5. Fold the flour in with a large metal spoon and spoon the batter evenly into the two prepared cake tins.
6. Bake for 20 minutes.
7. Take it out and allow to cool for 5 minutes. Peeling away the nonstick baking paper.
8. Whip the cream to soft peaks as the cakes cool, then coat the bottom half of the cake with the cream in an even layer.
9. Spread the strawberry jam on top of the cream. Sandwich the cake with the other half of the cake and put it on a serving plate. Sprinkle with the icing sugar and enjoy it.

CLASSIC SCONES WITH JAM AND CLOTTED CREAM

Prep Time: 10 minutes, Cook Time: 15-20 minutes, Serves: 5

INGREDIENTS:

* 250 g self-raising flour
* 120 ml 7-up / sprite
* 120 ml whipping cream
* 50 g caster sugar
* To serve: Jam and clotted cream
* To glaze: Milk or egg wash.

DIRECTIONS:

1. In a mixing bowl, combine together flour, lemonade, sugar and cream. Be careful not to overmix.
2. Dredge some flour on a flat surface and knead the dough.
3. Cut individual scones with a scone cutter.
4. Place scones in the basket with a 2 cm space between them.
5. Move slider to Air Fry/Hob, select Air Fry. Brush scones with milk or egg wash and cook at 180°C for 18 minutes.
6. Remove from the pot. Let cool for 5-10 minutes. Serve with jam and clotted cream.

APPENDIX 1: 28-DAY MEAL PLAN

Meal Plan	Breakfast	Lunch	Dinner	Snack & Dessert (Optional)
DAY-1	Margherita Pizza with Veggies	Chicken Thighs and Roasted Carrots	Moroccan Lamb and Lentil Soup	Vanilla Oat Apple Crisp
DAY-2	Baked Grapefruit and Coconut	Garlic Beef with Broccoli	Mashed Sweet Potato	Vanilla Spiced Quinoa Pumpkin Bake
DAY-3	Banana Breakfast Bars	Thyme Lamb Chops	Buttery Lemon Cod over Couscous	Classic Victoria Sponge Cake
DAY-4	Baked Egg and Avocado	Proper English Cottage Pie	White Bean Cucumber Salad	Healthy Crackers with Sesame Seeds
DAY-5	Stress-free Full English Breakfast	Authentic Cornish Pasties	Crispy Fish and Chips	Dates, Spelt and Sultana Biscuits
DAY-6	Baked Vanilla Fruit Granola	Sloppy Joes on the Buns	Homemade Easy Roasted Vegetables	Nutty Lemon Oatmeal Cacao Biscuits
DAY-7	Cheesy Courgette Pancake	British-style Pig in Blankets	Spiced Courgette Dish	Coconut Chocolate and Date Biscuits

Meal Plan	Breakfast	Lunch	Dinner	Snack & Dessert (Optional)
DAY-8	Baked Vanilla Bean and Cinnamon Granola	The Classic Steak and Kidney Pie	French Dip Beef Sandwich	Vanilla Oat Apple Crisp
DAY-9	Best Homemade Scotch Egg	Tempeh Onion Stuffed Cremini Mushrooms	Cranberries, Almonds and Wild Rice Salad	Sweet Blueberry and Chia Seed Vanilla Cobbler
DAY-10	Oatmeal Stuffed Apple Crumble	Baked Chicken Stuffed with Collard Greens	Buttery Lemon Cod over Couscous	Healthy Crackers with Sesame Seeds
DAY-11	Rainbow Vegetable Breakfast Hash	French Chicken Soup	Tempeh Onion Stuffed Cremini Mushrooms	Crispy Onion Rings
DAY-12	Jamaican Jerk Vegetable Patties	Buttery Salmon with Green Beans and Rice	Tomato Mushroom Stuffed Aubergine	Classic Victoria Sponge Cake
DAY-13	Herbed Breakfast Bean Sausage	Cheesy Ham Chicken Cordon Bleu with Green Beans	Beef Shepherd's Pie	Spiced Party Mix
DAY-14	Classic Scones with Jam and Clotted Cream	Roast Beef with Carrots and Onions	Homemade Christmas Dinner	Cheesy Garlic Pea Arancini

Meal Plan	Breakfast	Lunch	Dinner	Snack & Dessert (Optional)
DAY-15	Easy Yorkshire Pudding	Mediterranean Fish Stew	Cheesy Scallop Potato and Onion	Quick Crisps
DAY-16	Rainbow Vegetable Breakfast Hash	Cherry Pork Tenderloin	Bean and Turkey Chili with Rolls	Loaded Smashed Potatoes with Bacon
DAY-17	Herbed Breakfast Bean Sausage	Homemade Pot Beef Roast	Mediterranean Fish Stew	Fried Crispy Dumplings
DAY-18	Easy Baked Chickpea Falafel	Flavourful Chicken Stew	Farro and Strawberry Salad	Vanilla Spiced Quinoa Pumpkin Bake
DAY-19	Healthy Courgette Baked Eggs	Jerk Pork with Beans and Rice	Healthy Bubble and Squeak	Garlic-Jicama Chips with Scallion Cashew Dip
DAY-20	Margherita Pizza with Veggies	Seafood Paella	Olive and Beef Empanadas	Coconut Chocolate and Date Biscuits
DAY-21	Banana Breakfast Bars	Beef Shepard's Pie	Real Welsh Rarebit	Vanilla Oat Apple Crisp

Meal Plan	Breakfast	Lunch	Dinner	Snack & Dessert (Optional)
DAY-22	Baked Grapefruit and Coconut	Corn Chowder with Spicy Prawn and Bacon	Lemony Black Rice and Edamame Salad	Crispy Fish and Chips
DAY-23	Jamaican Jerk Vegetable Patties	Pork Tenderloin with Peppers and Potatoes	Lancashire Lamb Hotpot	Crispy Onion Rings
DAY-24	Baked Vanilla Bean and Cinnamon Granola	Bean and Turkey Chili with Rolls	Roasted Courgette Lasagne	Sweet Blueberry and Chia Seed Vanilla Cobbler
DAY-25	Spelt Banana Walnut Bread	Pho with Prawn	Moroccan Lamb and Lentil Soup	Easy Yorkshire Pudding
DAY-26	Maple Oat Coconut Flax Granola	Quick Ginger Chicken Pho	British Gammon Steak, Egg and Chips	Dates, Spelt and Sultana Biscuits
DAY-27	Baked Egg and Avocado	Beef Wellington with Mixed Mushrooms	Homemade Easy Roasted Vegetables	Nutty Lemon Oatmeal Cacao Biscuits
DAY-28	Oatmeal Stuffed Apple Crumble	Shredded Buffalo Chicken	Homemade Christmas Dinner	Classic Victoria Sponge Cake

APPENDIX 2: MEASUREMENT CONVERSION CHART

WEIGHT EQUIVALENTS

METRIC	US STANDARD	US STANDARD (OUNCES)
15 g	1 tablespoon	1/2 ounce
30 g	1/8 cup	1 ounce
60 g	1/4 cup	2 ounces
115 g	1/2 cup	4 ounces
170 g	3/4 cup	6 ounces
225 g	1 cup	8 ounces
450 g	2 cups	16 ounces
900 g	4 cups	2 pounds

VOLUME EQUIVALENTS

METRIC	US STANDARD	US STANDARD (OUNCES)
15 ml	1 tablespoon	1/2 fl.oz.
30 ml	2 tablespoons	1 fl.oz.
60 ml	1/4 cup	2 fl.oz.
125 ml	1/2 cup	4 fl.oz.
180 ml	3/4 cup	6 fl.oz.
250 ml	1 cup	8 fl.oz.
500 ml	2 cups	16 fl.oz.
1000 ml	4 cups	1 quart

TEMPERATURES EQUIVALENTS

CELSIUS (C)	FAHRENHEIT (F) (APPROXIMATE)
120 °C	250 °F
135 °C	275 °F
150 °C	300 °F
160 °C	325 °F
175 °C	350 °F
190 °C	375 °F
205 °C	400 °F
220 °C	425 °F
230 °C	450 °F
245°C	475 °F
260 °C	500 °F

LENGTH EQUIVALENTS

METRIC	IMPERIAL
3 mm	1/8 inch
6 mm	1/4 inch
1 cm	1/2 inch
2.5 cm	1 inch
3 cm	1 1/4 inches
5 cm	2 inches
10 cm	4 inches
15 cm	6 inches
20 cm	8 inches

APPENDIX 3: NINJA FOODI TIME TABLE

Pressure Cooking Chart

INGREDIENT	WEIGHT	PREPARATION	TIME
POULTRY			
Chicken breasts	900 g	Bone in	15 mins
	6 small or 4 large (about 900 g)	Boneless	8–10 mins
Chicken breasts (frozen)	4 large (900 g)	Boneless	25 mins
Chicken thighs	8 thighs (1.8 kg)	Bone in/skin on	20 mins
	8 thighs (900 g)	Boneless	20 mins
Chicken, whole	1.8–2.2 kg	Bone in/legs tied	25–30 mins
Turkey breast	1 breast (2.7-3.6 kg)	Bone in	40–50 mins
MINCED MEAT			
Minced beef, pork, or turkey	450-900 g	Minced (not in patties)	5 mins
Minced beef, pork, or turkey (frozen)	450-900 g	Frozen, minced (not in patties)	20–25 mins
RIBS			
Pork baby back	1.1–1.6 kg	Cut in thirds	20 mins
ROASTS			
Beef brisket	1.3-1.8 kg	Whole	1½ hrs
Boneless beef chuck-eye roast	1.3-1.8 kg	Whole	1½ hrs
Boneless pork butt	1.8 kg	Seasoned	1½ hrs
Pork tenderloin	2 tenderloins (450–700 g each)	Seasoned	3–5 mins
STEW MEAT			
Boneless beef short ribs	6 ribs (1.3 kg)	Whole	25 mins
Boneless leg of lamb	1.3 kg	Cut in 2-cm pieces	30 mins
Boneless pork butt	1.3 kg	Cut in 2-cm pieces	30 mins
Chuck roast, for stew	900 g	Cut in 2-cm pieces	25 mins
STEW MEAT			
Eggs	1–12 eggs	None	4 mins

INGREDIENT	WEIGHT	PREPARATION	TIME
VEGETABLES			
Beetroots	8 small or 4 large	Rinsed well, tops & ends trimmed; cool & peel after cooking	15–20 mins
Broccoli	1 head or 900 g	Cut in 2-4-cm florets, stem removed	1 min
Brussels sprouts	450 g	Cut in half	1 min
Butternut squash (cubed for side dish or salad)	550 g	Peeled, cut in 2-cm pieces, seeds removed	2 mins
Butternut squash (for mashed, puree, or soup)	550 g	Peeled, cut in 2-cm pieces, seeds removed	5 mins
Cabbage (braised)	1 head	Cut in half, core removed, sliced in 1-cm strips	3 mins
Cabbage (crisp)	1 head	Cut in half, core removed, sliced in 1-cm strips	2 mins
Carrots	450 g	Peeled, cut in 1-cm pieces	2–3 mins
Cauliflower	1 head	Cut in 2-4-cm florets, stem removed	1 min
Collard greens	2 bunches or 1 bag (450 g)	Stems removed, leaves chopped	6 mins
Kale leaves/greens	2 bunches or 1 bag (450 g)	Stems removed, leaves chopped	3 mins
Potatoes, red (cubed for side dish or salad)	900 g	Scrubbed, cut in 2-cm cubes	1–2 mins
Potatoes, red (for mashed)	900 g	Scrubbed, whole, large potatoes cut in half	15–20 mins
Potatoes, Russet or Yukon (cubed for side dish or salad)	900 g	Peeled, cut in 2-cm cubes	1–2 mins
Potatoes, Russet or Yukon (for mashed)	900 g	Peeled, cut in 2-cm thick slices	6 mins
Potatoes, sweet (cubed for side dish or salad)	450 g	Peeled, cut in 2-cm cubes	1–2 mins
Potatoes, sweet (for mashed)	450 g	Peeled, cut in 2-cm thick slices	6 mins
Runner beans	1 bag (350 g)	Whole	1 min

INGREDIENT	WATER	COOK TIME
GRAINS		
Arborio rice	750 ml	7 mins
Basmati rice	250 ml	2 mins
Brown rice, short/medium or long grain	300 ml	15 mins
Coarse cornmeal	875 ml	4 mins
Coarse oatmeal	750 ml	11 mins
Jasmine rice	250 ml	2–3 mins
Khorasan wheat	500 ml	30 mins
Millet	500 ml	6 mins
Pearl barley	500 ml	22 mins
Quinoa	375 ml	2 mins
Quinoa, red	375 ml	2 mins
Spelt	625 ml	25 mins
Sushi rice	375 ml	3 mins
Wheat berries	750 ml	15 mins
White rice, long grain	250 ml	2 mins
White rice, medium grain	250 ml	3 mins
Wild rice	250 ml	22 mins
LEGUMES		
Black beans	1.5 L	5 mins
Black-eyed beans	1.5 L	5 mins
Borlotti beans	1.5 L	3 mins
Butter beans	1.5 L	1 min
Cannellini beans	1.5 L	3 mins
Chickpeas	1.5 L	3 mins
Haricot beans	1.5 L	3 mins
Lentils (green or brown)	500 ml	5 mins
Lima beans	1.5 L	1 min
Pinto beans	1.5 L	3 mins
Red kidney beans	1.5 L	3 mins

* All grains should be 220 g amount, cooked by high pressure and released by natural (10 mins) then Quick.
* All beans, except lentils, should be soaked 8–24 hours before cooking, cooked by low pressure and released by natural (10 mins) then Quick.

Steam Chart

INGREDIENT	AMOUNT	PREPARATION	COOK TIME
VEGETABLES			
Asparagus	1 bunch	Whole spears	7–15 mins
Broccoli	1 crown or 1 bag (350 g) florets	Cut in 2-4-cm florets	6–9 mins
Brussels sprouts	450 g	Whole, trimmed	8–17 mins
Butternut squash	700 g	Peeled, cut in 2-cm cubes	12–18 mins
Cabbage	1 head	Cut in half, sliced in 1-cm strips, core removed	6–12 mins
Carrots	450 g	Peeled, cut in 2-cm pieces	7–12 mins
Cauliflower	1 head	Cut in 2-4-cm florets	5–10 mins
Corn on the cob	4 ears	Whole, husks removed	4–9 mins
Courgette	450 g	Cut in 2-cm slices	5–10 mins
Kale	1 bag (450 g)	Trimmed	7–10 mins
Potatoes	450 g	Peeled, cut in 2-cm pieces	12–17 mins
Potatoes, sweet	450 g	Cut in 1-cm cubes	8–14 mins
Runner beans	1 bag (350 g)	Whole	7–12 mins
Spinach	1 bag (450 g)	Whole leaves	3–7 mins
Sugar snap peas	450 g	Whole pods, trimmed	5–8 mins
Yellow courgette	450 g	Cut in 2-cm slices	5–10 mins
EGGS			
Poached eggs	4	In ramekins or silicone cups	3–6 mins

* All vegetables need 500 ml water and eggs need 250 ml.

Air Crisp Cooking Chart

INGREDIENT	AMOUNT	PREPARATION	OIL	TEMP	COOK TIME
VEGETABLES					
Asparagus	1 bunch	Halved, stems trimmed	2 tsp	200°C	8–10 mins
Beetroots	6 small or 4 large (about 900 g)	Whole	None	200°C	45–60 mins
Broccoli	1 head	Cut in 2-4-cm florets	1 Tbsp	200°C	10–13 mins
Brussels sprouts	450 g	Cut in half, stem removed	1 Tbsp	200°C	15–18 mins
Butternut squash	450-650 g	Cut in 2-4-cm pieces	1 Tbsp	200°C	20–24 mins
Carrots	450 g	Peeled, cut in 1-cm pieces	1 Tbsp	200°C	14–16 mins
Cauliflower	1 head	Cut in 2-4-cm florets	2 Tbsp	200°C	15–20 mins
Corn on the cob	4 ears, cut in half	Whole ears, husks removed	1 Tbsp	200°C	12–15 mins
Courgette	450 g	Cut in quarters lengthwise, then cut in 2-cm pieces	1 Tbsp	200°C	15–20 mins
Kale (for crisps)	1.5 L, packed	Torn in pieces, stems removed	None	150°C	9–12 mins
Mushrooms	200 g	Rinsed, cut in quarters	1 Tbsp	200°C	7 mins
Peppers (for roasting)	4 peppers	Whole	None	205°C	25–30 mins
Potatoes, russet	700 g	Cut in 2-cm wedges	1 Tbsp	200°C	22–25 mins
	450 g	Hand-cut fries, thin	½–3 Tbsp rapeseed	200°C	20–25 mins
	450 g	Hand-cut fries, soak 30 mins in cold water and pat dry	½–3 Tbsp rapeseed	200°C	24–27 mins
	4 whole (150-200 g)	Pierced with fork 3 times	None	200°C	32–37 mins
Potatoes, sweet	900 g	Cut in 2-cm chunks	1 Tbsp	200°C	15–20 mins
	4 whole (200-250 g)	Pierced with fork 3 times	None	200°C	37–40 mins
Runner beans	1 bag (350 g)	Trimmed	1 Tbsp	200°C	8–10 mins
POULTRY					
Chicken breasts	2 breasts (350–650 g each)	Bone in	Brushed with oil	190°C	25–35 mins
	2 breasts (220–350 g each)	Boneless	Brushed with oil	190°C	22–25 mins
Chicken thighs	4 thighs (200–300 g each)	Bone in	Brushed with oil	200°C	24–28 mins
	4 thighs (150–200 g each)	Boneless	Brushed with oil	200°C	16–22 mins
Chicken wings	900 g	Drumettes & flats	1 Tbsp	200°C	24–28 mins
Chicken, whole	1 chicken (1.3–2.2 kg)	Trussed	Brushed with oil	190°C	55–75 mins
Chicken drumsticks	900 g	None	1 Tbsp	200°C	20–22 mins

Air Crisp Cooking Chart

INGREDIENT	AMOUNT	PREPARATION	OIL	TEMP	COOK TIME
BEEF					
Burgers	4 patties, 80% lean (120 g each)	2-cm thick	None	190°C	10–12 mins
Steaks	2 steaks (220 g each)	Whole	None	200°C	10–20 mins
PORK & LAMB					
Bacon	1 strip to 1 (450 g) package	Lay strips evenly over edge of basket	None	165°C	13–16 mins (no preheat)
Pork chops	2 thick-cut, bone-in chops (300-350 g each)	Bone in	Brushed with oil	190°C	16–19 mins
	4 boneless chops (170-220 g each)	Boneless	Brushed with oil	190°C	15–18 mins
Pork tenderloins	2 tenderloins (450-650 g each)	Whole	Brushed with oil	190°C	25–32 mins
Sausages	4 sausages	Whole	None	200°C	8–10 mins
FISH & SEAFOOD					
Crab cakes	2 cakes (180-220 g each)	None	Brushed with oil	175°C	8–12 mins
Lobster tails	4 tails (80-120 g each)	Whole	None	190°C	7–10 mins
Prawn	16 jumbo	Raw, whole, peeled, tails on	1 Tbsp	200°C	7–10 mins
Salmon fillets	2 fillets (120 g each)	None	Brushed with oil	200°C	10–13 mins
FROZEN FOODS					
Chicken nuggets	1 box (350 g)	None	None	200°C	12–13 mins
Chips	450 g	None	None	180°C	18–22 mins
	900 g	None	None	180°C	28–32 mins
Fish fillets	1 box (6 fillets)	None	None	200°C	13–15 mins
Fish sticks	1 box (400 g)	None	None	200°C	9–10 mins
Mozzarella sticks	1 box (300 g)	None	None	190°C	6–9 mins
Pot stickers	1 bag (10 count)	None	Toss with 1 tsp rapeseed oil	200°C	11–14 mins
Pizza rolls	1 bag (550 g, 40 count)	None	None	200°C	12–15 mins
Popcorn Prawn	1 box (450 g)	None	None	200°C	8–10 mins
Tater tots	450 g	None	None	180°C	19–21 mins

APPENDIX 4: RECIPES INDEX

T

W

Printed in Great Britain
by Amazon